The Incredible Ditch

Some of the Workers
Who Built the Middlesex Canal

Nathan Adams

Daniel Allen

James Ashley, stone work

Joshua Atwood, carpenter

John Austin

John Austin Jr.

Moses Austin

William Ayers

James Baldwin, master carpenter

Ebenezer Ball, blacksmith & stone work

Isaac Barker

John Bateman

Thomas Bennett

Solomon Blood

Levi Boles

Reuben Boles

Asa Bootman

John Bowers, stone work

Richard Briggs, stone work & other

Elephalet Brown

Josiah Brown

Levi Brown

Francis Burnham

Jonathan Burnham, blacksmith, stone layer

John Butler

Samuel Butterfield

Thomas Butterfield

William Butterfield

James Calwell

Hiram Cannon

Simeon Cannon

David Capen, stone work

John Caswell

David Chambers

John Chandler

Roger Chandler

John Chapman

Timothy Clough, stone layer

William Clough

Daniel Clyde

Hezekiah Coburn

Loammi Coburn

Medad Combs

James Conery

John Crosby

Samuel Dale

Aaron Davis

Phineas Davison, stone work

Samuel Dow

Henry Dowing

Benjamin Dowse

Benjamin Dowse Jr.

Samuel Durant

Reuben Durront

John Eaton, stone layer

Robert Elmwood

Abraham Emerson, master stone layer

John Emerson

Jonathan Emerson, stone work

Timothy Emerson

Caleb Farley

Joseph Farley

Moses Farnum

Silas Farwell

Samuel Fay

Aaron Fletcher, carpenter

Oliver Fletcher, stone work & other

John Ford

John Fox

James Francis

Isaac French

Abial Frost

Samuel Fry

Stephen Gage

Joseph Gardner

Daniel Gault

Abraham Gibson

Samuel Gilman

William Gordon

Daniel Got

Daniel F. Gregg

Thomas Guy

Peter Hadley

Richard Hall

Asa Hardy

Francis Harris

William Haskell

Nathan Hastings

William Hide

James Hildreth

Timothy Hill Jr., carpenter
Nathan Hoar
Isaac Hobart, stone layer & master workman
Jacob Hobart, stone work
Edward How
Barnett Hughes, carpenter
John Humbolt
Nathaniel Hunt
Timothy Hunt
Ezra Ide
William Jay
David Jewell
John Johnson, stone work
Reuben Johnson, blacksmith, stone work
Samuel Johnson
Zachariah Johnson
Peter Jones
Zebediah Jones
John Kean
Morris Kelley
James Kelly, stone work
Davids Kendall
Joseph Kendall
Nehemiah Kidder
Abner Kimball
Ebenezer Kimball
Joseph Kinney
Joseph Lane
Daniel Lawrence
Levy Leach, stone work
Nathaniel Levermore, stone layer
William Little
Isaac Lund
Oliver Lund
James Lunds
John Mahaney
Jesse Manning
Jonathan Manning
Timothy Manning
Jonathan Marbel, carpenter
Thomas Marshall
John McKee

Philip Mills
Andrew Moore
Benjamin Needham
Samuel Noyes, carpenter
John Osborn
Daniel Page
Ezekiel Page
William Park
Amos Parker
John Parker
Lemuel Patterson
Lemuel Patterson Jr.
Edward Pettie
Richard Pettie
David Pettingill
William Pettingill
John Phelps
Simeon Phelps
Stephen Pierce
Elijah Pilsbury
Joseph Pittingill, stone layer
Eliphalet Poore
William Preston
Ebenezer Reed
Daniel Richardson
William Richardson, carpenter
William Richey
Samuel Rideout, stone work
Charles Ripley
John Robbinson
John Rogers
Joseph Ryan
Benjamin Sanderson
John Scottow
David Searle
Jacob Shaw
Jacob Shed
John Shipley
John Shirley
Jacob Silver, master workman in stone laying
John Smalley
Thomas Smith

Joeseph Snow, stone work
Putnam Spaulding
Zachariah Spaulding, carpenter
Moody Spofford
Samuel Spofford
Samuel Sproke, Jr., carpenter
Erastus Stanton
Osgood Steel
Aaron Stevens
Samuel Steward
Oliver Stiles
Benjamin Swain
Daniel Swallow
David Tarbell, carpenter
Jonathan Tarbell
Joseph Tarbell, blacksmith, stone work
Joseph Tallant
Peter Taylor
Joseph Tenny
Jonathan Thompson
Herbert Thorndeck, stone work, digging at the
locks
William Todd
George Tufts, carpenter
Jeremiah Tyler
Ebenezer Varnum
Nathan Webster
Nathan Webster Jr.
John Weeks, carpenter
John Whittle
Samuel Wilder, stone work
Henry Willard, stonework
David William
David Wilson
Elijah Wilson
James Wilson
Asa Winn, stonework
Joshua Wirt
Abel Witherbee, stone layer
Joshua Wright
John Wyman

The Incredible Ditch

A Bicentennial History of the Middlesex Canal

by Carl and Alan Seaburg
and Thomas Dahill

The Anne Miniver Press
for the
Medford Historical Society
Medford, MA
1997

Text by Carl and Alan Seaburg
Artwork by Thomas Dahill
Book design by Suzanne Morgan

Dedication

To Fran and Burt VerPlanck

for their many contributions to the Middlesex Canal Association over 50 years (25 years each!)
and their remarkable gift of caring attention to the old canal.

Sponsors and Patrons

These individuals and institutions made major gifts to make the publication of this book possible.

We are most grateful for their encouragement and support.

Sponsors

The Medford Historical Society

The Middlesex Canal Association

Tufts University

Thomas W. Lincoln

Patrons

Dr. John M.R. Bruner and Barbara Temple Bruner

In memory of the family of William E. and Anne (MacLean) Creamer,
including William Jr., Ronald, Constance, and Carolyn

In memory of John and June R. Griffin by their son Jay B. Griffin

Maria C. Von Magnus Henderson

Audrey Leary

Mayor Michael McGlynn

Dorothy J. Norris

In memory of Agnes E. Peterson by her family

Fran and Burt VerPlanck

In memory of Pasquale Volpe, and Angelo and Angelina Volpe

Medford Bank (*formerly* the Medford Savings Bank)

Medford Cooperative Bank. In memory of John Hand by Robert Surabian

Acknowledgements

Especially to Jay Griffin and the late Dr. Joseph Valeriani of the Medford Historical Society who supported this project from its beginning. To Noah Dennen, treasurer of the society who has handled the finances of the project, to Michael Bradford curator, and especially to Caesar Fittante who will be handling the mailing and shipping: to all these we are most grateful.

To the many people in the Middlesex Canal Association, including Nolan Jones, Thomas Raphael, Leonard H. Harmon, David Dettinger, Betty Bigwood, Marion Potter, Jane Drury, Betty Bigwood, Fred Lawson Jr., Arthur Louis Eno Jr., Roger Hagopian, Wilbar Hoxie, Burt VerPlanck, and Frances VerPlanck.

To Sally Pierce, Boston Athenaeum; to Ms Tamulonis and Ms Wendy Haynes of The New-York Historical Society.

To the invaluable research of William Corbett and the late Harry Condon.

To Martha Mayo and Janine Whitcomb at the Mogan Center Library in Lowell.

We are greatly indebted to Tom Smith and Kathleen O'Doherty of the Woburn Public Library. Tom has been most responsive to all our many inquiries.

To Kevin Shupe of the Manchester (NH) Historic Association and Jane Porter of the Portsmouth Athenaeum. To Charles Mower who answered endless questions.

To David Soule and Robert Flynn.

To Marcia Folsom who helped us in the hunt for the IAA papers and slides.

To all who aided our Trolley Car Hunt, especially Margaret Ingraham and Alexander Ingraham.

To Peter Woodbury of the Billerica Historical Society, and Thomas F. Harkins of the Duke University Archives.

To the Society for the Preservation of New England Antiquities for supplying us with the Baldwin Coolidge photos.

The gracious cooperation of so many people in this project has been much appreciated.

With special thanks to Suzanne Morgan for her fine work in designing this book.

Introduction

The Medford Historical Society is celebrating during the 1996/1997 season one hundred years of preserving the history of Medford. Among many other events marking this special occasion, we are sponsoring this book recognizing the bicentennial of the Middlesex Canal.

The connections between the Middlesex Canal and Medford are close and deep. The earliest supporters for a canal linking Boston with the Merrimack River were Medford citizens like Andrew, Benjamin, Ebenezer Sr., Ebenezer Jr., and Willis Hall, Samuel Swan Jr., and Jonathan Porter - farmers, merchants, landowners, the prominent worthies of the village.

In the beginning, Medford was to be the natural terminus of the canal. Boats and barges would continue down to Boston by the Mystic River. Later, when the canal was extended to Charlestown, the Medford supporters pushed for a direct connection to the river. So the branch canal was built in 1804. This made it possible for lumber from New Hampshire forests to come immediately into the village for the use of the new ship-building industry. This important industry flourished in Medford for a quarter of a century after the passing of the canal.

Brick from the Medford brickyards went up the canal and helped to build mills in Lowell and New Hampshire. And who knows how many private houses up-country were built with these same bricks which came out of Medford's claypits? Thus the Middlesex Canal played a significant part in Medford's economic history during the nineteenth century.

So it is altogether fitting that in celebrating our one hundredth year, we should be sponsoring this bicentennial history of the Middlesex Canal.

Although most traces of the canal have long since been erased or built over, we in Medford have not forgotten the ingenuity and industry of our forebears in helping to build this canal. We remember its important contributions to the canals that were later constructed based on the technology pioneered here. And in reading and looking at the illustrations in this book, perhaps we will recover a sense of the nostalgia and pleasure that our ancestors knew in voyaging on the old canal in the "good old days."

Jay B. Griffin
President, Medford Historical Society
April 1997

Contents

Acknowledgments ❖ x

Introduction ❖ xi

A Jaunt to Horn Pond ❖ 3

Bringing New Hampshire to Boston ❖ 13

How the Canal Was Born ❖ 23

Diary of a Dig ❖ 31

Taming the Merrimack ❖ 47

How the Canal Worked ❖ 57

Overview ❖ 65

Overflight ❖ 73

Closing Down the Canal ❖ 87

A Canal Scrapbook ❖ 95

Afterglow—Since Closure ❖ 113

New Life—New Interest ❖ 121

Sources ❖ 131

Index ❖ 135

The Incredible Ditch

A Jaunt to Horn Pond

What better to do on a hot summer day than to take a cooling jaunt into the countryside on the Middlesex Canal? So on Friday, July 18, 1817, my father, Josiah Quincy, hitched up our carriage and gig and soon the seven of us were jig-jogging over the bridge to Charlestown. We were headed for Beachum Landing on the Mill Pond where the canal packet boats leave for Lowell. We had been invited by Superintendent John Sullivan to join a party of friends who were going to spend the day at that noted pleasure resort, Horn Pond up in Woburn.

What a lot of activity we find at the Landing! Hand trucks loaded with boxes were being wheeled to and from the barges. Carriages were arriving and departing with passengers. Rafts of lumber were floating lazily in the mill pond. The chatter and clatter made my head spin!

What a lot of our friends were already here! Surely there's more than fifty. There was the distinguished lawyer Daniel Webster and his wife. He's only recently moved to Boston and settled into his law practice. And the Sullivans and the Winthrops. We seven Quincys. Ralph Waldo Emerson's cousin George. Eliots and Buckminsters and a gaggle of handsome young men from Harvard

College to add spice to the outing. And swarms of children. For certain it's going to be a lively party.

How colorful the packet boat looks, brightly painted white, with red and black stripes, and light blue posts. After gingerly climbing into the boat—it rocks slightly in the canal waters as we step aboard—we took a peek inside the cabin. It's large and comfortable with upholstered seats, and painted a cheerful orange, We could sit there but it's too nice a day to be inside, so we walk forward and sit under the shade of an awning. Soon the two horses that are to pull the boat are brought along and harnessed to a rope from the boat. Then we start, ever so gently; the horses walk along the canal path drawing us easily and smoothly after them. It's just half past nine when we depart.

The boat enters a lock that separates the canal proper from the Mill Pond. The gates shut and we are closed in a damp wooden box. It's as if we were at the bottom of a mouldy chest. But just ahead of us water comes sizzling down from above, and gradually we find ourselves rising in the world. Finally we come to quite a respectable height, the gates are swung open, and we move forward into the canal.

The canal swings around the base of Ploughed Hill where the advance lines of the patriots were entrenched when Boston was

Facing page - The Charlestown mill pond, 1805

besieged. If you let your imagination run free you can still see them up there this July day just as they were in 1775. What would they have thought of a canal boat passing right through their lines!

Looking over to our right we can see the Mystic River sparkling in the sun with several small craft sailing up and down. To our left we can see the inland part of Charlestown with its pretty farms and houses. Cows are browsing in the pastures, and the fields are green with growing crops. Birds wing in the air above us, and the wind rustles in the branches of the trees along the canal. The reeds and bulrushes along the edge of the canal sway in the breeze. As we glide along we see a young lad fishing from the canal bank.

"Caught anything?" we shout to him. With a grin the boy holds up a fat trout.

People are strolling about on the packet boat, stepping into the cabin for a moment or two, then out on to the deck again. Soon we pass through the magnificent estate that once belonged to the late Colonel Isaac Royall. The great house gleams in gray and white some distance over on our left and some of the servants can be seen busy on their various employments in its gardens and grounds.

Someone remarks that George Washington visited this house during the Revolution and that Colonel Stark from New Hampshire made it his headquarters when our troops were surrounding Boston. Lately it has been restored to Colonel Royall's heirs. How surprised General Washington would be to think that one day people would sail almost by the front door of this elegant mansion!

Soon the canal bends left just beyond the branch canal built to give timber easy passage down to the Medford shipyards. For a time we glide fairly near the Mystic River. Then the canal turns right and we cross over that river on a bridge of water! They call this an aqueduct. Our host, Mr. John L. Sullivan, tells us it is 135 feet long. What fun to rush to the sides of the boat and look down on the surface of the river some ten feet below us! What amazing times we live in when our engineers can make one river pass over another!

Now our boat comes to another lock in the canal. As we approach, the Captain blows his horn to let the lock tender know we are coming. Mr. Sullivan tells us that this is called Gilson's Lock, named after the lock keeper. Slowly the boat edges its way into the lock which is just slightly larger than the boat itself. Then the gates at the end by which we entered are closed, and wickets opened in the upper gate. Gradually the lock fills with water, gently lifting our boat some ten feet. What a delightful sensation as bit by bit we rise out of our dank, dark surroundings to the level of the land around us. And all so effortlessly and almost silently.

The gate keepers and his assistant hop over to the upper gates and open them so we can continue on our way. The canal route now takes us through the grounds of that eminent Boston merchant Peter Chardon Brooks. The banks on either side are beautiful with his gardens, trees, and fields full of growing plants. It is a temptation to step off the boat and stroll along under their shade, but we resist.

As the horses tow us leisurely on we can see over to our left the ruffled surface of Mystic Pond. The sun glinting on its waters seems to be winking at us between the trees along its shore. And now the canal swings left as if to go right into that lake, but instead we find our packet is crossing over the Symmes river that feeds the lake. We are in another long wooden aqueduct that carries us safely to the land on the opposite side. Mr. Sullivan tells us this aqueduct is 180 feet in length and needs constant repair!

Crowd at Charlestown landing

After this engineering marvel, our boat encounters another, the Gardner Locks, which are two locks not one. This time some of us disembark and stroll about during the time required to lift our boat to the next higher level of land. Some of the young men pick wildflowers growing along the tow path to present to the ladies.

Reboarding, we soon come to a bridge with the odd name of Huffmaster's Bridge. Mr. Sullivan tells us a curious story about this Huffmaster who was said to have been a Hessian soldier during the Revolutionary war fighting for the British but later settled here. He was considered rather peculiar. People remembered him wearing knee breeches made of eel skins and a coat braided out of corn husks. Odd he was, said Mr. Sullivan. Indeed I should think so!

"Are there eels in the canal now, Mr. Sullivan?" pipes a squeaky voice.

"There sure are," he replies, "And clever boys like you sometimes catch them and bring them home to Mother to cook up for dinner They're. mighty tasty, too!"

Our boat silently slips under the bridge and drifts along through a level plain. Here and there a farmhouse can be seen in the distance. It is pleasant to look out on the cultivated fields and to enjoy the slight breeze our slow passage brings us. The boat wends its way around a hill and through a wood beside a little stream on whose further bank stands a mill.

Once more the captain blows his horn as we approach Hollis Lock. There we see "a passing pond" as Mr. Sullivan calls it. Here boats can wait if the lock is occupied, or unload if this is the end of their journey. Then we go under one more bridge and just before us is our destination, the Lake of the Woods or Horn Pond.

This lovely lake is surrounded by hills covered with stately pines and other trees. In the middle of it is a small wooded island.

We go through one of the Stoddard Locks and then come to a basin where our packet boat anchors and we eagerly disembark. Just behind us, looking out to the lake is Horn Pond House, a grand inn known for hospitable entertainment of canal-men and passengers. We could go there, but decide to walk over to the open Pavilion situated nearer the lake. Here one has a fine view. We can faintly hear from across the lake, strains of music coming from the island.

Shortly, a boat full of musicians leaves the island and rows across to the Pavilion. Playing their instruments joyously, they march, followed by our frolicking youngsters, to a high spot between the canal and the lake. Here the ground is more level and the grass had been cut. An awning is stretched over this cleared area. Many people gather up here and the band plays while the children dance.

Suddenly one of the boys notices a canal boat full of passengers coming down from Lowell to Boston through the upper locks. There is a great deal of waving and shouting back and forth, and then they continue on to Boston. Finally, the band plays a lively march and we all go down to the Pavilion where an excellent cold dinner is spread out for us. When we can't eat any more, it's back to the dancing and games and strolling about.

Too soon it's late in the afternoon. "Time to start back," shouts the captain. So with the band leading the way we reluctantly enter the boat and set out. Tables were placed the whole length of the boat on which were arranged fruit, wine, ice, and glasses. Mr. Sullivan had thought that it would delay us too long if we had our desert at the Pavilion. The band tootles away and occasionally people break into songs as we retrace our way homeward.

By the time we reach Mystic Pond, some people think we left too early so once again the boat stops, people get off and with the band giving us a lively marching tune, we make our way through

Horn Pond house (Linscott)

the woods down to the shores of the pond. Off in the distance we can see the spires of the churches in Arlington. As we are walking by the lake, some of the young ladies spy a great profusion of fragrant and colorful water lilies growing just a short distance offshore.

There arises a great clamor from them for water lilies. "We must have them!" "Who will fetch them for us?" But alas, they are just too far out of reach to get them without getting wet.

Up speaks the gallant Daniel Webster. " Is there no gentleman spirited enough to come forward and get them? Is no one gallant enough?" It was as if he were addressing some great throng or a jury. You cannot imagine how eloquent and persuasive his voice is!

"Strange! 'Tis very strange! If I were a young man the ladies should not ask for those flowers in vain." Webster is all of an elderly 35! "If I was as young as I was a few years ago I would ransack the shores of the Pond until I found some boat or boards by which to reach out and gather those lilies."

How impressive Webster can be! Thus challenged, the college lads, not to found lacking in chivalry, all bound off at top speed in search of a boat All but two. Samuel May and George Emerson held back.

We began to reproach them, but the two friends had a surprise up their sleeves. They were only waiting until the other lads were out of sight. Then, Sam and George wade out into the lake up to their chests, gathering armfuls of the flowers to bring back to us.

"A little further, gentlemen," says Mr. Webster, "there is another on your right, and one on the other side, over there." I beseech Mr. Webster not to urge them further. "Oh," says he, "it does not hurt young men to get their feet wet. I would have gone myself were it not for the ladies."

Shortly the young lads are back with the flowers and present them to Mr. Webster. From him we ladies each receive one. Mr.

Sullivan came up just then and asked the lads what had induced them to do it.

"Ah, sir," replies young May, "it would have required more courage not to have done it after the challenge we received. I claim no merit, Sir. The ladies owe these lilies less to my gallantry than to Mr. Webster's eloquence. I could not stand unmoved by his appeal!"

"Never before," replies Webster, "Have I gained a lily by my eloquence."

Showing that Harvard students have a bit of the old blarney themselves, May responds, "Perhaps not, but your eloquence has often been crowned with laurels."

Then we shower our two heroes with praise and thanks, and concern that their dripping clothes might imperil their health. Even the gentlemen commend them for their manly endeavor.

It was at this moment that the other young men came back along the shore of the lake, dragging an old dory which they had found about a quarter of a mile away. We gather to greet them, each lady with a lily in hand or bosom or on her head, and even the gentlemen swinging some. The future Sons of Harvard are quite bewildered until they noticed Sam and George's wet pantaloons. Light dawns. The dory is forgotten. They surround the two traitors threatening them with a quick and just retaliation. Now we ladies enter the fray determined to protect our gallant heroes. The only penalty Emerson and May .pay for their gallantry was that they have to wear their wet pantaloons the rest of the afternoon!

My mother, Mrs. Eliza Quincy, walks up the bank by Mystic Pond and seats herself on the stump of a tree. Some of the younger men gather round her feet and she sings several songs for them.

Sailing by the Royall House

At length a return to the boat is sounded by the band, and we all march through the woods to that popular tune, "How sweet through the woodlands."

Back aboard the packet we float idly down the canal, stopping at Gilson's lock to have coffee served to us aboard the boat from the nearby tavern. While the boat is "locked down," the children dance a cotillion on the grass. Then our homeward journey is resumed. By now the sun had set, the moon was rising, and with the band playing jaunty tunes and the gentlemen singing merrily away, we float peacefully the four miles back to the Mill Pond in Boston.

What a wonderful day we all have had. We jog on home, delighting in our pleasant memories and treasuring our water lilies.

Gathering lilies in Mystic Lake

Bringing New Hampshire to Boston

This was the day! This was the day! Young Hosea hadn't slept more than a wink during the night for yesterday Pa had said "Yup" to his going down the canal to Boston market with the pine logs that he, Uncle Harry, and Hosea's older brother Massena had just finished cutting in their wood lot. So immediately the sun gave a hint that it was in the east Hosea, just ten days away from his eleventh birthday, tossed aside his colorful patchwork quilt, jumped out of his bed, grabbed the clothes he had laid out the night before, stuck them under his nightshirt, and ran out to the barn.

Here he talked his Pa's two oxen into standing up and moving away from their soft hay bed so he could dress in its warmth. Then he dashed through the cool morning wind into the fragrant kitchen and his breakfast of pancakes and sausages.

Their raft, about 75 feet long and 9 1/2 feet wide, had been put together the day before with the wedges that held the logs securely together His Pa had named the raft for his wife Ruth and her name with the number one as was required by the canal authorities was painted on a board on the right side of the raft. Hosea sat excitedly on the logs while Pa stood at the back of the raft to

Using wind and current on the Merrimack

steer. Massena and Uncle Harry put up a sail, and they glided smoothly down the river at a good clip.

His Pa called out to Uncle Harry, "Can you see Old Hildreth?" "Nope," Harry replied. "Good," said his Pa.

"Who's old Hildreth?" Hosea asked Massena.

"It's not a he, it's a rock," replied Massena."If you can't see it, that means the river is high enough so that you don't need to pass through the side canals and pay the toll. You can take the river all the way down to the Middlesex Canal at no cost. It saves a lot of time."

His Ma's tasty pancakes along with the wonders of Concord in their home state New Hampshire, and the starting point of Hosea's first incredible adventure, had long ago popped out of his head for every bend of the river brought a fresh experience and he was sure the best was still to come.

The swift breeze soon brought the raft and its passengers to where they could enter the Middlesex Canal. On their right was Massachusetts and the country town of Chelmsford. His father's mind, now, was on the immediate task of navigating the heavily loaded raft through the three locks linking the river to the canal. The locks, about eighty feet in length, were at Middlesex Village, from which was to develop in a few years the great mill city of Lowell.

Hosea's father with the help of his brother and oldest son, and shouts and cheers from his youngest, steered the raft from the river into the semicircular basin which was the entrance to the canal. It was about two hundred feet wide, twelve feet deep, and reached maybe a hundred feet in from the Merrimack.

Once that was accomplished Hosea's father with a glance at the two on the bank called to his youngest son, "Let's say we have some of the food your Ma prepared while we wait our turn to enter the lock." And they did just that!

As they ate they all examined the first lock of the canal which was dead ahead. Adjoining it were two more. Hosea's eyes nearly popped out of their sockets. Each lock was built of stone and was about 80 feet long; the last two had paddle-gates on each side which when opened allowed the water to flow into the lock below. Soon the gates in the first were opening to let a loaded scow out and when it was the lock keeper motioned to another raft and the *Ruth* to come into the lock. Then he swung the gates shut and as the water gradually flowed in the rafts slowly rose to the level of the next lock. When they were finally level with the canal they were 25 feet above the Merrimack. Hosea was amazed and turned his head to smile at his Pa who winked back.

Before they could go further, Uncle Harry had to talk with the gate keeper and get their "passport" for travel on the canal. This document was one of the canal requirements and had to be shown at every lock and signed by the man on duty there. Once in Charleston it had to be returned at the Collector's office and the proper toll paid. Only then could a boat be unloaded at the wharf. Next, they had to hire a horse to pull the raft down the canal. With that done they started for Boston.

The canal now took them under the main street of the Vil-

Hosea waking up

Facing page - Putting the raft together

Passing Shawsheen aqueduct (Joseph Payro)

lage, crossed over the Black Brook by a wooden aqueduct which was ten feet above the flowing bubbling water, crossed yet another Village street, and then led them through a great marshy area called the Great Swamp which divided the Merrimack and Concord rivers from each other. Uncle Harry and Massena had their work cut out for them to keep the horse at its task on the tow path especially as the raft was maneuvering the Black Brook aqueduct. But they did. Hosea didn't know if he should be riding on the raft or running on the towing path and ended up doing a little of each.

Soon the raft with its load of pine timber reached a second aqueduct about half the length of the first one. This was called the River Meadow or Hale's Brook aqueduct. A couple of miles ahead was the town line between Chelmsford and Billerica and soon afterward there was the stone guard lock which was the entrance to the Concord River millpond at Billerica. This was the summit of the canal, 107 feet above tide-water at Charlestown, and 25 feet above the Merrimack River. The Concord river was the main source of water for the canal, supplemented if needed by Horn Pond in Woburn.

The scenery along here was a pleasing mixture of trees and meadows. The tall Lombardy poplars with their green leaves especially caught Hosea's fancy. Then he looked into the water to see if he could see bottom. Yup he could. Heck he thought it's not very deep, I could jump in and my head would still be above water. But he didn't dare because he knew his Pa would be cross.

It was nearing seven o'clock and since canal traveling at night was forbidden except on moonlit nights and this night there would only be a quarter moon, the older men were considering where to tie up for the evening. Perhaps they could do so with permission at the mill pond. If they rose early tomorrow Uncle Harry thought they should make their destination before the sun set.

That was what they did and the next morning they were all up with the roosters. Hosea started the day not riding the raft but walking along the tow path with his brother and the horse. The sun rose pretty he thought and he began whistling.

"Massena."

"Yup." His older brother liked to imitate their Pa.

"How do they keep the canal bank from caving?" And he pointed to a small hole just below the surface of the water. He had noticed several yesterday and they had puzzled him. Indeed he found everything about the canal curious and exciting. Maybe when he got older he could be a lock tender on a canal. Maybe he could even be the skipper of one of the big canal boats he had heard about.

"Patch it."

"How?"

"With straw." Massena laughed and stopped playing Pa. "That hole you saw Hosea was made by some animal. A muskrat or maybe a mink. Uncle Harry says they have men who just walk the canal banks to patch the holes. Maybe that's a job for you," and he laughed again. Hosea smiled at him and they continued behind the horse both whistling now.

When they neared the much talked about Shawsheen Aqueduct Hosea hopped back onto the raft which was clearly the place to be now. Their raft approached the Shawsheen River and the canal aqueduct over it through a stretch of lovely meadow edged by purple asters. As they neared it Hosea noted that the canal was now running along on an embankment above the much lower surrounding meadow. At this point Pa had to stop the raft in the basin before the aqueduct because there was a packet boat in front of them and the rule of the canal was that only one boat could go through the aqueduct at a time. That was okay with Hosea because it gave him a chance to study how the aqueduct had been made.

The ground had been built up on either side of the river to about eleven times his height of three feet and the aqueduct itself was almost two hundred feet long. On either of its ends it was held up by a stone abutment and between these were three more stone piers each supported by wooden braces. Running from one embankment to the other and through the piers were long, large pieces of timber. These had been laid horizontally to strengthen the aqueduct but also to serve as a base for the canal itself which was shaped by them and by its wooden sides. The passage created was very narrow which was why only one boat could use it at a time. As he watched the packet boat maneuver the aqueduct Hosea could hardly wait until it was their turn to go through.

It was as much fun as he had hoped it would be. First the horse tended by his brother went along the tow path slowly pulling the raft. The rope between it and the raft was taut. His Uncle walked behind. Hosea kept glancing at the water in the canal, then at his Pa steering, next at the horse, and then at the Shawsheen River so far below. This was the most exciting thing that had ever happened to him and he kept reliving it during the rest of the day as the raft proceeded on its way.

Within half a mile they went through another lock, Nichol's Lock, and then after another mile and a half they crossed over the Lubber Brook by the Sinking Meadow Aqueduct, but it was such a small one that Hosea thought it was an insult to even call it an aqueduct.

At Gillis' Lock, when the lock tender came out of his house and spotted Hosea sitting on one of the logs on the raft he called out for him to jump to the tow path and let him ride the front gate as it swung open and then shut. Since there was a canal tavern here, and since they were at the half way mark of the Middlesex

Throwing apples at the horse

Canal, Hosea got to watch the raft while his father, Uncle Harry, and Massena visited it for something cold to drink. When they returned Pa brought Hosea a glass of icy spring water from the lock tender's wife.

Then the raft continued on its merry if bumpy way until the canal suddenly made a dramatic and sharp bend, the Ox-Bow bend Pa called it, to avoid passage through a swampy meadow. As interesting as everything seemed to Hosea nothing compared to the Shawsheen Aqueduct as far as his lively imagination was concerned.

As they were moseying along through Wilmington, the horse began to tire. Then he spied some fragrant grass along the tow path and stopped to sample it.

Hosea's father called to him,"Get some of those fallen green apples over there and plug them at the horse. That'll get him going again."

Hosea and his brother gathered up armfuls of the apples, went to the front of the raft, and found it great fun to fling the apples at the horse. Sure enough, Pa was right, it got his attention quickly and he forgot the grass and settled back into his slow but steady walk.

Soon they had left the country town of Wilmington in the distance and were approaching North Woburn where, running back from the canal Hosea saw the handsome gardens and the impressive mansion of Loammi Baldwin. Pa had told him that it was once the home of the engineer who had built the canal. Hosea would have liked it if Pa and Uncle Harry would stop here so he could see it better but they were intent on getting to Boston before darkness arrived as neither wanted to spend another night on the canal. They were also anxious to sell their timber and get back to their farms.

Junt then a horn sounded. Hosea looked up as it blew again.

Going by Baldwin mansion (Linscott)

"Pa," he shouted with excitement, "there's a boat coming up behind us." Pa nodded; he had seen it for some time and knew that when it was about to overtake the *Ruth* the boatman would sound his horn as required by the rules for traveling on the canal.

Pa gave some instructions to his brother and older son and the raft slowed down. They took out their poles and pushed the raft away from the towpath side of the canal, letting the tow rope drop into the water. "On the canal, Son," he said to Hosea, "boats always have the right of way over rafts." The boat passed smoothly by them, Pa and the men on the boat exchanging greetings. Hosea was all smiles as he waved to the boat's crew. The captain responded by sounding his horn one more time. Then things settled back to where they had been.

So on went the raft patiently pulled by the horse on the tow path toward Horn Pond and its three double locks which caused the canal to drop an amazing fifty feet. Well, amazing at least to young Hosea. Horn Pond, or as his Uncle Harry always called it, the Lake of the Woods because around its shores were hills and tall pines, was one of the most popular spots on the canal and Hosea was startled but glad too when one of the boats tied up in the basin before the inn there blasted its horn in greeting to the raft. He and Pa waved in return.

Once through a couple of more aqueducts found the raft close to the Mystic Lakes in West Medford and soon going under the gracefully arched stone bridge on a farm there. Hosea wished that they had such a handsome bridge on their farm in New Hampshire. Maybe Pa would let Massena and he build one. Certainly there was enough stones to do so on their land. But he didn't think about it very long for there were so many other exciting sights catching his eye.

An aqueduct took them ten feet above the Mystic River and then they were passing another large mansion, the Royall House.

Pa who had worked in Boston when he was a young man and knew lots of tales told him the house was very old and was built many years ago. "Before we fought the British?" "Yup." The house was a wonderment. Around it were several outbuildings, a pasture with cows and even an orchard. Hosea, however, was glad he didn't live there. He liked his own house and his own small comfortable bed better.

Now they were traveling now through the town of Charlestown and were very near the end of their two day trip. On the left were marshes and on the right some hills. Hosea noticed several willows bending over the canal and nodding as if they were half asleep. They were quite different looking than the Lombardy poplars he had seen yesterday just below Middlesex Village.

Then they were at Lock No. 1 and Landing No. 1 in Charlestown. Here the waters of the canal flowed into an ancient Mill pond which the canal company now owned and where they had constructed offices, storehouses, a smithy shop, a lock tender's house, a packet wharf, and booms to hold the timber brought down from New Hampshire and elsewhere. The Mill pond bustled with activities and was filled with rafts, boats, logs, and ship spars. While Hosea and Massena stayed with the raft and its cargo, Pa and Uncle Harry went to the Collector's office with their Passport and paid their toll and landing fees. This accomplished, Pa and Uncle Harry arranged to have the timber surveyed and then negotiated its sale.

"Let's have something wet," exclaimed Uncle Harry and they did at a nearby tavern, even Hosea who was allowed a couple of glasses of apple cider. Then Pa took them over to Boston. They saw the Common, the State House, the Charles River, Cornhill, the harbor, and even got to walk out on Long Wharf. Two nights later Hosea was back home curled up in his bed with his patch work quilt pulled over his head. Visions of aqueducts, locks, and packet boats were dancing in his head as he drifted off to sleep.

Blanchrd House, Medfad

How the Canal Was Born

Judge James Sullivan Remembers

*N*ow that the Middlesex Canal has been completed and is operating as we had planned, perhaps it would be useful for me, as President of the Canal Corporation, to set down for posterity why this canal came into being.

At the end of the Revolution, we Americans looked around and saw that the country now belonged to us. We were exultant with our new freedom and everywhere we looked we saw great opportunities for our country. Among these were canals. England and France had canals. Many of them. But there were only a few in the new United States. And those did not go any great distances.

What is a canal? Basically it is a artificial river made by people. This river goes where people want it to go. It has almost no current, no rocks, no rapids. It is level, except where boats using it need to be lifted up or down to another level in containers called locks.

Why is a canal? Having been born in the District of Maine in 1744, and trained as a lawyer in the law office of my brother, I can tell you exactly why canals are important. How often when I was a lawyer in Maine I had to ride circuit on horseback along our rough roads cut through the wilderness. Later when I be-

Blanchard House in Medford

came a judge in Massachusetts, again we had to take stagecoaches over terrible roads to attend court in the various counties of the commonwealth.

What canals do for you is smooth out the passage. They turn a rough trip into a pleasant, gentle boat ride. And for transporting goods they are far superior to the roads we have even today. On our roads, one strong horse could draw at most a ton of goods. On a canal the same horse could draw 25 tons, at a constant speed, with no time-consuming struggle uphill, and no danger that coming down the hill the brakes might give way and the wagon run upon the horse, or be upset, and the horse injured or killed.

One yoke of oxen on a canal can draw up to 100 tons of goods. Eighty teams would be needed to transport the same amount on land. Nor is there mud to contend with in rainy seasons on canals. And the time saved in the whole process, made canals far superior to the overland roads presently available.

Where canals can go was also a major consideration. Before canals, cities had to depend on rivers. New York had the mighty Hudson River reaching far into its interior, Philadelphia had the Delaware, Portsmouth had the Merrimack, Hartford had the Connecticut. Boston had only the Charles and the Mystic, both reaching just a few miles out of town.

What Boston needed was canals. As we looked at a map there were three obvious places where canals could help Boston trade expand. If we cut a canal across Cape Cod it would save ships the long and dangerous passage around the arm of the Cape. If we could build a canal to connect with the Connecticut river we could tap into the goods and trade of that state and Vermont, and perhaps even reach up to the St. Lawrence river and Canada. Or if we could have a short canal up to the Merrimack river that would open up the interior of New Hampshire to trade with our merchants.

My idea was that some kind of a canal to the Merrimack might be the cheapest and quickest for us to build as a start. As I studied the inadequate maps we had, it seemed we could take advantage of the natural rivers and lakes, and only need to build a few locks and stretches of canal where there were not navigable streams.

The more I looked at the maps the more possibilities I saw. We could continue up the Merrimack using locks to bypass its rapids, till we got to Concord, New Hampshire. Then the Warner river might give us access to Lake Sunapee, and further rivers might take us over to the Connecticut River. If the Winooski River could be reached by a length of canal our boats could then enter Lake Champlain and proceed up into Canada where another small canal could connect us with Montreal. Perhaps we could even have side canals on the Concord and Nashua rivers!

My head was giddy with the possibilities that would open up. Canadian trade could come directly to Boston without the dangerous outside passage down the St. Lawrence River, then around and down the coast. But the first step towards all this was to connect Boston with the Merrimack River.

Judging from the poor maps we had this seemed possible. The Mystic River went from Boston up to Medford. At its head were lakes, then a boat could go up the Symmes river through to Woburn. A short canal might connect us to Horn Pond. There if we could hook up with the Concord River in some fashion, we would have an easy passage into the Merrimack.

Our first survey by an untrained local surveyor revealed that there would have to be some necessary changes in that plan. The second survey, by the skilled English surveyor, Mr. Weston, gave us a more accurate route and enabled us to settle on a western route for the canal.

But before either of these surveys were made, we had gathered together a small group of interested people. I had consulted on this idea with Colonel Loammi Baldwin, an old friend, then serving as sheriff of Middlesex County. Like me, he had long been interested in canals. He became as enthusiastic as I was about our project.

Since the terminus of the canal as originally conceived would be in Medford, we brought a number of the leading citizens of that town into our confidence. They too saw the possibilities for their town. At this time I was serving as attorney-general for the Commonwealth, and having earlier served in the legislature, knew the proper steps to get ourselves incorporated as a corporation. We became one of the first public corporations.
Accordingly, we presented a petition to the legislature early in November 1792. I had added one or two other important names (like James Winthrop, another Judge) to our list. Altogether 13 of us signed the petition. It passed the House in February and was agreed to in the Senate a month later. We advertised it in one of the Boston newspapers in April, and on June 22, 1793, Governor John Hancock formally signed the Act. As a public utility we were also given the right of eminent domain. This was unusual.

It was now necessary for us to organize, sell shares in the enterprise, hire a person to oversee the construction and begin to make our dream canal real. We met soon afterwards and a committee including Baldwin, Winthrop, and two of the Hall brothers of Medford were authorized to have a survey made. Because

Governor John Sullivan

of my lame left leg from a childhood accident, I thought it advisable not to go tramping around the countryside myself. And since I have a touch of epilepsy now and then, I had to consider that too.

But this did not mean I sat around doing nothing. I was on the committee charged with getting subscriptions, and we had 800 shares to sell. Shares were priced at an initial two dollars a piece, but it was fully understood that there would be further assessments made upon the shares to support the work as it progressed.

Once the first survey by Mr. Samuel Thompson had been made and a report of it published in the Boston papers, we set out looking for subscribers of an enterprising kind who shared our view on the necessity for a canal. It was surprising how quickly we sold the shares.

I was gratified that many of our leading citizens bought shares in the canal: men like President John Adams and his son John Quincy Adams, Benjamin Joy, Christopher Gore, Joseph Barrell, Peter C. Brooks, the Hall family, Samuel Parkman, the Warrens, the Parkers, and all the good old Boston names - Winthrop, Weld, Wendell, even Abraham Touro down in Rhode Island. And Governor John Hancock bought 20 shares that September, though he died barely a month later.

The proprietors of the canal met on October 7, 1793 at 10 o'clock in the morning at the Blanchard Tavern in Medford. The next day Governor Hancock died. The Proprietors elected me president, and so I have continued even after I became Governor in 1807 and was reelected this present year 1808.

In 1795 we went back to the legislature and got an additional act passed on Feb. 28, 1795, which allowed us to attach other canals to the Middlesex Canal if it seemed appropriate. This act authorized us to use the Concord River as far as Sudbury for canal purposes, to improve the banks of the Mystic River to render the canal easy and useful, to open a canal around the shallows of

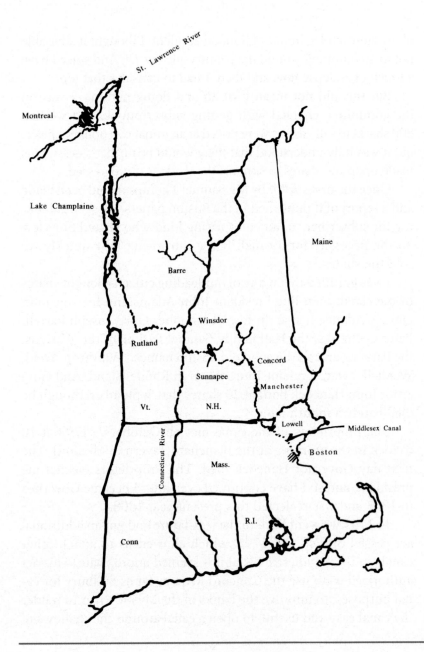

the Merrimack river in the town of Dunstable, and to extend the Middlesex canal from Medford to the waters of the Charles River or Boston.

I was looking at a map that we had Osgood Carleton prepare in 1795 based on the survey Thompson had done. It showed the contrasting claims of an eastern route through Stoneham and Wakefield, and a western route through Woburn and Wilmington. Quite clearly this shows that the canal we envisioned at the beginning of our enterprise was not the canal we finally built.

The Thompson/Western versions showed in effect three canals. One canal ran from the Merrimack River to the Concord Millpond. A second canal ran from the millpond to Horn Pond in Woburn. Boats would then cross Horn pond and enter a third canal that discharged them into the Aberjona River. From here boats would proceed down the river into the Mystic Lakes and then by way of the Mystic River into Boston. Was this wise?

This was an important consideration since some of the Boston merchants who were now serving as directors of the canal were asking that we bring the canal directly into the Boston area, rather than ending in Medford. A canal that came overland directly to Charlestown could be used by boats any time of the day, and not depend on the tidal flow of the Mystic river.

This question continued to be agitated for a number of years, until finally by 1800 a decision was made to extend the canal through Medford into Boston, and not to use Horn Pond, but have the canal run alongside it. In other words, one canal for the whole distance from the Merrimack River into Charlestown millpond.

This decision meant that we began buying land in Medford in 1802 to use for canal purposes. We did not buy the Charlestown millpond until 1803.

Potential canal route from Boston to Montreal

This decision did not please some of the Medford proprietors. An industry in building ships on the banks of the Mystic had begun in 1803. They wanted New Hampshire lumber dropped off on their doorstep and not first sent into Boston and then laboriously have to be transhipped back up the Mystic to the shipyards. So it was decided to permit them to construct a branch canal in Medford that connected our canal to the Mystic river in order to serve the needs of the local merchants and shipbuilders.

Colonel Baldwin had begun as early as November 1793 to buy land for the canal. This required skillful negotiating on his part. He dealt with over 100 landowners during this time. Most of the land came to the corporation through voluntary sales. In sixteen cases we had to use the eminent domain authority that had been granted to us by the legislature. Land prices ranged from around $150 per acre in Medford to $25 per acre in Billerica. I prepared all the conveyances myself.

Our stock was seen as valuable property and what had originally sold for $2 per share by the fall of 1794 was selling for $25. By the time the canal opened in 1803 a share cost $473 and by 1805 it was selling for $500 per share.

Colonel Baldwin ordered a set of surveying instruments from London for us to use and we received those in October 1794. They cost us $163.35.

Once they started building the canal, I noticed that they were using a cart on the canal to remove the dug earth, but it seemed inadequate to the purpose, so I contrived one better fitted for the job. It had solid timber wheels 24 inches in diameter and 18 inches long on the axle. The cart body itself was 4 feet by 6 and the bottom of the cart about 30 inches off the ground. The whole would be about 6 feet high. It could be backed under the projecting earth to be removed, so that when the dirt was tipped by an iron bar, it would fall directly into the cart, thus saving labor with the spade to fill it. I found that my early experience in farming came of practical use in matters like this.

Colonel Baldwin built a sample cart following my description, albeit with some modifications and improvements, and it soon proved very successful and saved the workers much labor.

In early 1803 Colonel Baldwin, after so many constructive labors on behalf of the canal, became discouraged with the constant supervision of the proprietors. He informed me that he was ready to resign. Knowing what an appalling effect this would have on our whole enterprise, now so nearly completed, I wrote him assuring him that there was no distrust or discontent in the minds of the Directors with his work as an artist; that they had never had, even for a moment, a want of confidence in his attachment to the project, nor any doubt as to his integrity. I pleaded with him, since we are so near the end of the project, to pursue the enterprise to its rightful conclusion, one that will bring honor and laurels to all our brows. Fortunately, Colonel Baldwin acceded to my most sincere request. The work on the canal proceeded until the job was completed on Dec. 31, 1803 - exactly within the terms of our contract.

If Colonel Baldwin had been having his difficulties about the canal, I must admit that I myself was also beginning to have some secret doubts. Could we possibly make it a financial success? Since the weather would not permit us to operate the canal throughout the whole year, it meant that we should receive less tolls that we had projected. Would they be sufficient to cover the interest on the capital expended?

I began to fear that they might not. Perhaps our sanguine hopes might be disappointed; and what is still more mortifying was that we might be made the instruments of disappointment to our friends. But the future will have to show whether my doubts have any solid foundation.

For the present, all seems fine. As the Colonel and I wrote in our February 1806 report to the proprietors on the operation of the canal in its second full year things seemed most promising. We determined that over 9,405 tons of merchandise had been transported down to Boston on the canal a distance of 27 and a quarter miles. If these items had been carried overland at the standard hauling price of 25 cents, it would have cost $53,484. On the canal the tolls would have been $13,372, but because we wished to encourage the lumber business we charged them less, so the tolls actually came to only $11,832. This amounted to a savings of $41,652 to the owners of the goods, and much cheaper prices for consumers.

If these goods had been carried by land, it would have required 9,405 teams of four oxen, one cart, and one man a day and a half each. Thus the labor of 14,104 days of a man, the labor of 56,430 oxen, and the wear and tear on 9,405 carts over a day and a half were saved to the public. This meant goods could be sold for much less, and with less damage to the articles themselves. It was disappointing that only a small quantity of goods were being transported on the canal from Boston into the country, only 308 tons in 1805. There can be no doubt that the owners of salt, sugar, molasses, iron, and other heavy goods, could have saved themselves three quarters of the expenses of transportation if they had used the canal. Our efforts will be bent to convince them of the value of using the canal both for the outward movement of merchandise to the countryside as well as for its importation into Boston.

After the resignation of Colonel Baldwin in 1806, Samuel Jaques was made the Agent of the canal. He was succeeded by my son John Langton Sullivan in 1808 as Agent. It gave me great pleasure to see that my interest in this important project would be continued by my own flesh and blood.

Note by James Winthrop: Governor Sullivan died Dec. 10, 1808, in the sixty-fifth year of his age, and was buried with the honors conferred on his exalted station, and which were acknowledged to belong to his distinguished merit.

AMOUNT OF BUSINESS DONE ON THE CANAL IN THE COURSE OF THE YEAR 1805

Wood, 3997 cords, weighing	5000 tons
Oak Timber, 422 tons measure	422
Pine do., 1405 tons measure	1200
Oak Plank, board measure, 187,200	374
Pine Plank, 912 thousand, board measure, weighing	1100
Stone	310
Cyder, 3242 barrels	405
Ashes, 33 barrels	8
1848 empty hogsheads	42
2196 empty barrels	12
154 half barrels	2
360 kegs	3
36,920 hogsheads hoops	70
11 tons, 13 hundred & 23 pounds of hoops	11 3/4
Shooks	23 3/4
Hoop poles	1 3/4
Grain, 155 bushels	3 1/2
Apples, 493 bushels	5
Other articles	20 1/2
Sumack	2
3750 Clapboards	3 3/4
4569 Staves	5
147 thousand Shingles	29
77 barrels of Beef	9
237 bushels Flax Seed	6
Ranging Timber	5
1800 Rails	3
Goods carried up	308 1/2
	9405 tons

A printed notice from the Middlesex Canal Scrapbook,
Boston Public Library

Above - Amount of business done on the canal in 1805
Facing page - Turning over the first spadeful for the canal in Billerica

Diary of a Dig

Note: Loammi Baldwin was chosen to be the first superintendent of the Middlesex Canal. This meant he was responsible for the planning and construction of the whole enterprise. He kept an occasional diary, and this, plus his frequent letters, enabled us to put together a year by year summary of the progress and problems of building the Middlesex Canal. To a large extent this is in his own words.

The First year - 1793

After I was chosen superintendent for the canal, I had to hire someone to survey the best route for it between Medford and the Merrimark. I chose Samuel Thompson of Woburn, a self-educator surveyor, for the job. Benjamin Hall, Judge James Winthrop, myself, and my sixteen year old son Benjamin Franklin Baldwin accompanied him on this expedition which took us 9 days. We hired a chaise to carry our baggage and victuals. We stayed at 7 different taverns and our meals cost a shilling apiece.

We started at Medford bridge and carefully traced the course of the Mystic river which is largely serpentine. Either side of the river is mostly marsh. The course could easily be straightened if

---

Building the aqueduct over the Mystic River, Medford

---

necessary. As the tide rises to the mouth of Medford pond (or Mystic Lake), it seemed sufficient for loaded boats to pass at high water. The distance between Medford bridge and the Weir Bridge where the pond begins is about two miles and a half.

Two miles further brought us to the head of Medford pond. From thence by a winding stream we arrived in Woburn near the Black Horse tavern. We passed by Abel Richardson's mill dam and found a rapid in the stream near John Symme's house. This would be a proper place for a lock. About a quarter of a mile above Richardson's there is a stream which runs into Horn Pond in Woburn.

Our hope was to find a way into the Concord River by way of Bedford. We viewed the streams feeding Horn Pond, but found the meadows in which they rise to be surrounded by high hills. This is part of a ridge that stretches from Wilmington to Arlington. We finally found a valley from the mill through the east part of Woburn up to Wilmington that rose moderately to a meadow crossed by the Ipswich river. The river crosses the Andover road to Boston, not far from Dean's Tavern.

At Wilmington it is called Maple Meadow River, and runs through an extensive meadow. Crossing this and continuing on for about two miles we came to Jaques' mill in Wilmington. We followed a brook through extensive meadows to Sandy Pond. The rise of ground was about ten feet and an half. From there we passed by a valley of low upland to Beard's mill on the Shawsheen River. The valley is about two feet higher than Sandy Pond, but when we came to the bank of the Shawsheen it fell about two feet. The river's surface is about four feet below the pond, so the canal would have to pass over it on a short aqueduct. From here to the Concord river in Billerica is a bit more than three miles.

From here the obvious route of the canal drops down to the Merrimack River crossing Black Brook and an extensive meadow known as River Meadow in Chelmsford. Following the valley and passing east of a barn belonging to Mr. Bateman, we come to the Merrimack river at a single oak tree in the road near an oak stump.

Once we had this report in hand the Proprietors of the canal met to decide how to proceed. At the present time it is thought the cost of the canal may be not less than one hundred thousand dollars.

We were uneasy about the result of this first survey, particularly in the leveling instrument that Mr. Thompson used, so I met with General Knox and John Hills the surveyor, in Boston. As a result we worked with Mr. Cross who helped us make what we hoped was a better instrument for leveling. Using this new instrument, I spent five days, from October 21 to 26, with Samuel Jaques trying it out.

I was still dissatisfied with our results so we contacted General Knox now in Philadelphia to see if we could secure the assistance of a person from England skilled in the business of canaling whom we had heard was then in this country. In the meantime, I started buying land for the canal.

I also resigned as sheriff of Middlesex County in November, but agreed to continue in office until about the second week of January.

The Second Year - 1794

Last year was spent in organizing. Not one shovelful had yet been turned on the canal. This spring the proprietors asked me to go to Philadelphia to see if Mr. William Weston, the Englishman we had heard of, would come to our assistance. I bought a traveling trunk, picked up expense money from the treasurer, and on Monday, March 10, hired a man, horse, and chaise to take me to Boston. There I booked on Pease's stage for the Southern states to meet Mr. Weston.

I stopped off in New Haven and consulted with an engineer building a canal there. Then I took the packet to New York and again talked canals with people who had begun some in northern New York state. They had had little success and were most discouraging.

I went on to Philadelphia arriving on the 18th. I met Mr. Weston who is very eminent in his profession, but found he was working on two canal projects and a turnpike project. He would like to work for us, but does not see how he can.

Fortunately Mrs. Weston is with him and she has a passionate desire to visit Boston. She observed that all the English gentlemen and ladies enjoyed themselves better in Boston than any place on the continent. I declare that almost my only hope of securing Mr. Weston's assistance rests on this fortunate circumstance. I told him that if he would go with our company we would never leave him dissatisfied.

While he was deciding what to do, I took the opportunity to travel down to the Potomac to view the locks and canals being built there. When I returned I found Weston willing to spend some time in June to help us. The people he was working for granted him six weeks' leave of absence to help us. He loaned me a fine instrument to bring back with me that we can use for surveying

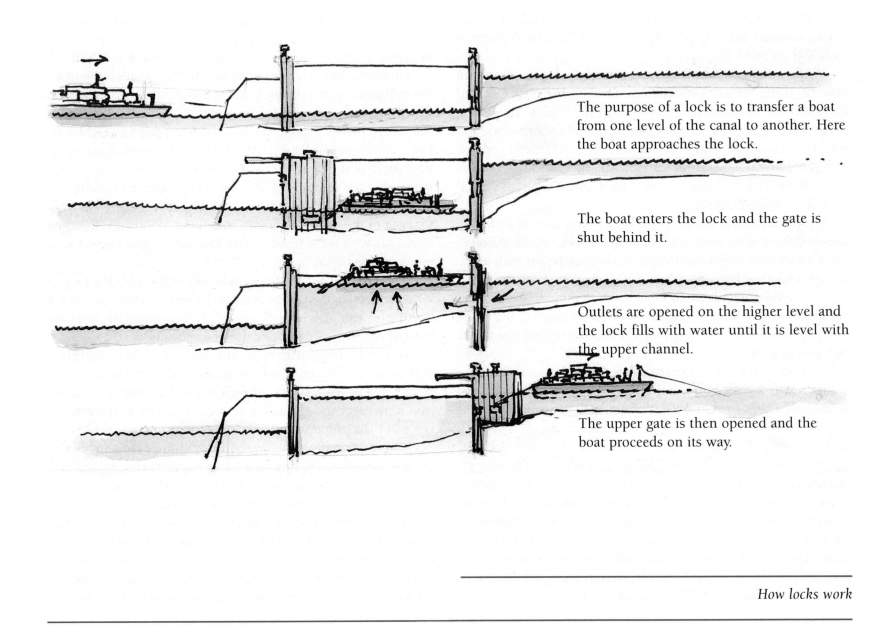

The purpose of a lock is to transfer a boat from one level of the canal to another. Here the boat approaches the lock.

The boat enters the lock and the gate is shut behind it.

Outlets are opened on the higher level and the lock fills with water until it is level with the upper channel.

The upper gate is then opened and the boat proceeds on its way.

How locks work

With Mr. Weston's agreement secured, I traveled back home, having covered some 1200 miles. I arrived back in Woburn at midnight on April 16.

While waiting for Mr. Weston to arrive I spent four days from May 12, using Weston's instrument, leveling between Concord River and the Merrimack. We completed the field work and the paper work by May 21. Samuel Jaques, one of the directors, and my two sons, Cyrus and Loammi, assisted me. Later I ordered additional instruments from London according to Mr. Weston's descriptions. In June I was elected to the General Court as a Senator from Middlesex county.

Weston arrived here July 13 and a few days later he and I, his assistant, three of my sons, and five others set out with three horses and a phaeton to begin our Ocular Survey. We began with a fine dinner at Ichabod Parker's tavern of roast chicken, lamb, and fried fish washed down with two double bowls of punch. I sent one of my boys back to Judge Winthrop's in Cambridge for the plans and papers of our former surveys. Then we settled about our business in earnest.

We made our headquarters in Billerica. For the next nine days, both afoot and with horse and chaise, we were busy. My sons assisted us. Cyrus carried the station staff and Benjamin Franklin the chain. Carefully we went over the entire route.

On August 2, Weston made his report. The main decision had to be between taking the canal on an easterly route through Reading and Stoneham, or on a western route through Wilmington. There was much opposition in Reading and Stoneham to the canal going through there and we had generous offers from the Wilmington people to assist us gratis on the dig, so we finally chose the western route. This looked to be the least costly and controversial of the two. It should be noted here that Mr, Weston estimated the cost of the canal to be between $350,000 and $450,000.

The proprietors authorized five of us to be a committee to stake out the route of the canal from Concord River to the Merrimack. We decided to begin our first work at that end.

On September 4 we began to lay out the canal at Billerica at the mill pond which the proprietors had purchased. On September 10 we broke ground for the canal. I turned the first spadefull. The sentence I spoke at this historic moment was, "May the Eye of Wisdom and the Eternal Mind aid this work designed for the benefit of the present & all Future Generations." Mr. Samuel Jaques dug the second sod, then my son Benjamin Franklin, and lastly Mr. Thomas Richardson. Next Mr. Jaques and I cut a sod for each of the absent directors, and Judge Winthrop closed the ceremony with these words, "May Providence give eternal prosperity to this Canal."

It was now necessary to begin hiring workers for the project. We advertised in the papers and sent people into the countryside looking for men. We hoped particularly to contract the work out to local people, and limit our use of foreigners.

There were few experienced canal builders in the United States at this time, so we relied as much as possible on the local yeomen. Many of the farmers through whose land the canal would pass were eager to help us out in order not only to increase the value of their property, but also for the advantage of ready cash. They were naturally experienced in draining fields, in digging ditches, in pulling stumps, and using animal teams. In addition, some sections of preparing the bed of the canal could be let out to contractors, who brought their own workmen with them.

We also erected a good blacksmith's shop with two forges which soon provided us with tools for the work. We had hired a master carpenter and he spent a month building wheelbarrows and making other needed equipment. The best foreign gunpowder we could find was purchased. We soon ran into an obstacle,

Colonel Loammi Baldwin

a rock formation, which required blowing up. Unfortunately, a premature explosion occured and four workmen were injured

The Third Year - 1795
We had begun digging so late in 1794 that only a little was acoomplished before winter set in. But once the ground thawed in the spring, work began in earnest.

Weston had sent us the dimensions for the canal last year even before he arrived here, and I wrote him that we were using his plan. The canal would be twenty feet wide at the bottom and thirty and a half feet wide at the top. It would be three and a half feet deep. The inclined angle of the banks was set at 33 degrees. The towing path would be one foot above the water, and ten feet wide. The bank on the opposite side the same height and five feet wide. The committee voted that the locks should be 75 feet long, but we have not yet decided whether they would be built of wood, brick, or stone. I asked Weston for directions in how to puddle the banks if that became necessary so that we would not lose water.

The directors decided that I would be in charge of digging the canal from Mystic Lake in Medford to Jonathan Beard's house in Wilmington and that Samuel Jaques would oversee the work from Beard's house to the Merrimack River. Jonathan Thompson would be in charge of making and constructing the locks of the canal. But from the nature of my employment actually all of this work fell under my oversight. At this time I had about one hundred men working on various sections of the canal.

During the summer I was planning and executing several bridges over the Concord River in Billerica. It was also necessary to secure bricks and begin preparations for several culverts in the Northern Department. I also had men preparing timber and planking for boats to be used in the Concord River for banking.

Meanwhile some of men in the Southern Department had

levelled the land for the canal from Horn Pond to the inlet of Mystic Pond and staked out the line that we shall follow there. We have broken ground in Paul Wyman's land, about half a mile south of Horn Pond and completed about 35 rods of the canal. About 34 men were working in this area. They also errected the frame for one sluiceway to drain the canal and have completed a blacksmith shop near Woburn meeting house which will answer for the whole Southern Department, particularly for the building of the locks at the descent into Horn Pond. I also have men out looking for stone to use in that construction.

There was a shortage of housing in the southern section of the canal so we built a mess house for fifty men on Paul Wyman's land. Jeremiah and Zeb Wyman to board workmen.

In late August I had to bail S. W. Harvey from prison. He had been put there for debt; the duties of a superintendent run the gamut. By September we had broken ground in Simpson's meadow, having nearly finished blowing out the only two ledges of rock there. I have been looking at two routes for the canal to the Merrimack River. The directors will decide which one we choose.

On October 6 we began work on a brick culvert in Billerica, and the next day we began to lay out the first lock at Chelmsford. Two weeks later the first load of stone for this lock came down by boat from Tyngsboro. The directors have ordered that I discontinue the work in Woburn for the time being. I am to concentrate on getting the work completed from the mill pond to the Merrimack. The men discharged from working in Woburn can work in Billerica if they choose. Jaques will have charge of them there. Some of the men were upset, particularly since I didn't have in hand the money to pay them. Some of the men went immediately to Billerica. Others stopped until I could borrow the money

Surveying for the canal

to pay them. During this period my situation was rather uncomfortable.

The season has been wet and discouraging, but the superintendents were united in making the attempt to get the northern branch of the canal operating. We had 73 workmen busy. They cut through the deepest hills in the Rogers land, and now are principally occupied in banking across the swamp on his land.

We put in a brick culvert, but had to keep the the pump working every half hour day and night for almost 10 days to keep the water out. Then there came a thunderstorm as we were finishing up and the rain overflowed the banks and broke into the work but without injuring any part of it.. We had to put down wooden pipes to help drain the swamp. Some of these will always be underwater and should endure a long time.

We finished a sluiceway below the Proprietor's mill, raised stone abutments for a bridge across the Concord by the mills, cut through the deep hills in a lengthy piece of ground in the Roger's land, and are about ready to let water into 2 and a half mile of the canal, after Mr. Dowse finishes 2 or 3 days of work there.

On December 16 we let the water into the canal for the first time from the Concord River as far north as Timothy Manning's. To our delight the water stood about 18 inches deep for about 2-1/2 miles. The level did not vary half an inch and the banks held well. On the 18th we let the water out again.

The Fourth Year - 1796

Weston sent me directions how to make the canal impervious to water leakage. Where the embankments are composed of sand and gravel and the like it would be necessary to ram the bottom and slopes of the canal with clay. The rams should be 5 feet long and at least 7 inches in diameter with a handle to hold them by. They made me think of the paddle in a butter churn. The clay

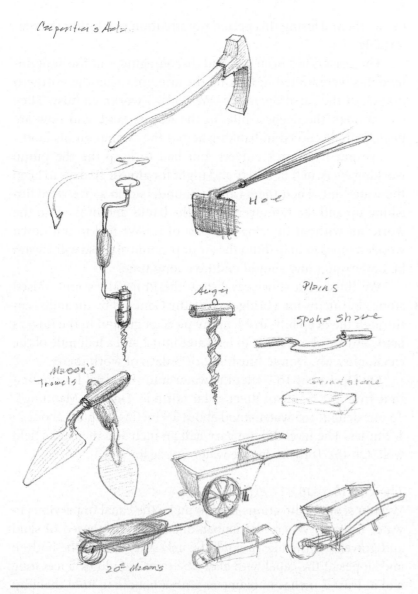

Sketches of tools used in construction of the canal

should be at least six inches thick in places that would be exposed to water. Once the clay was well rammmed into place, it should then be covered with another six inches of clay, rammed again, and so repeated until the whole had received a coat two feet thick. The clay coating should also be carried up on the banks. He also sent us a recipe to make an excellent and durable cement for use in the locks.

Since the locks at Merrimack Village were to be built of stone, it meant we had to use a hydraulic cement that would set under water. Weston advised us to use Dutch trass. This was a form of earth that could be found on the site of extinct volcanoes. Weston's recipe was to use two bushels of trass, one bushel of lime, and three bushels of river sand.

We heard that trass had been discovered in the West Indies so on June 16 a ship was sent to bring back a cargo. Forty tons of it arrived in Medford on August 22 and cost us $10 a ton. I sent it, a ton at a time, up to Chelmsford by wagon. The directors decided in August that we would use four parts of the trass to one part of slaked lime, but not add the sand. Only a little water was worked in. The whole was thoroughly beat before using. I found that this would harden under water in a few days to such a degree that you could not make any impression upon it with a thumb nail.

This year I had barracks built in the "Great Swamp" for some of the workers. Bunk beds were provided filled with straw. The rate for board was the same for all the workers, namely $2.00 per week. For this they were served bread, meat both fresh and salted, whatever vegetables were in season. Cider and beer were served at meal time. Occasionally fish replaced the meat. We also provided butter, sugar, chocolate, and the cheapest grade of Bohea tea. The cooks were instructed not to use more than four barrels of beer per month for each fifty men.

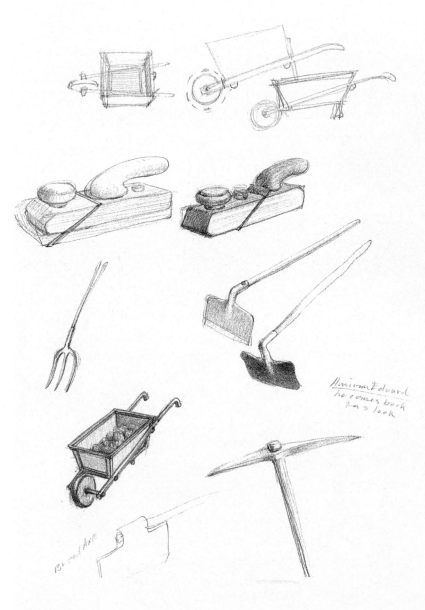

On Oct. 18 we opened the lock and canal at Merrimack River and the first lock broke and failed. A month later we finished the second lock there and it was more successful

The Fifth Year - 1797

As the year opened, no part of the canal was completed and open. We were constructing two aqueducts and three stone locks, but there was not a great deal to show for three years of effort. The directors insisted that we should at least finish the canal from Billerica to Middlesex Village by the end of the year, and our efforts will be bent to that goal.

In June a raft of timber came down from Mr. Blodget for the locks. This first raft he delivered was a good lot of timber but not all of yellow pine neither was it free of sap as the contract specified. A second raft was received at the end of July. The principal part of this raft was good timber but some sticks were bad. Very little part answered strictly to the description in the contract. I believe it was found much more difficult to fulfill the contract than was imagined at the time it was made.

By October work had progressed fairly well on the six mile section of the canal that the directors wanted me to publicly exhibit, but there were many doubts in my mind. The masonry had not dried properly, the mortar in the locks was unseasoned. It required exposure to water for some time. We had not constructed the stop gates yet. They only allowed me to postpone the demonstration two weeks.

When we allowed water to enter the canal from Concord River to the Merrimack for the demonstration, the banks in general appeared to resist the effect of the water beyond what was expected. However, the high embankments in the River Meadows threatened to give way, but we took a boat out of the Merrimack and applied it with a number of men to convey earth to the parts

most affected, so an actual break was prevented. The old well-seasoned base of these banks which had lain near two years added greatly to their support. They surely must answer very well when properly seasoned.

So on Nov. 9, we celebrated the work completed at the Merrimack end of the canal. That day, the directors and some other prominent citizens rode to Billerica. There we boarded two canal boats. Workmen, carrying the tools appropriate to their skills, walked on either side of the boats as they were towed by horses to a basin halfway to the Merrimack river. We stopped and, as the workmen cheered, christened this Sullivan's Harbor in honor of the president of our corporation, James Sullivan.

The boats then continued on accompanied by our marching troops and when we came to the aqueduct over the Black Brook, we stopped again. To my delight I have to report that they gave the name Baldwin to this aqueduct. Then we went on and the boats passed successfully through the first two locks, but the lead boat grounded on the floor of the last lock.

The problem with the breach in the last lock was caused by the violent motion of the water entering the lock when we had not fully completed the work on it. Even though the carpenter, blacksmith, and stone cutter were employed early and late and considerable work was done in the night time.

Despite this disappointing conclusion, all of us - workmen, directors, and guests - marched over to Howard's Tavern and put

away 150 pounds of roast beef, two bushels of potatoes, tasty gravy, plenty of bread, and a barrel of cider.

But also in November I had to report to the directors that of ten contracted jobs east of the Concord River that should have been completed by the early summer of 1796, only two were finished, and the rest less than half completed. There has been little work done on that section of the canal for about a year past.

The frost seems to be setting in, the tools are exposed by working in the frozen ground, the days are short, the Thanksgiving in New Hampshire has taken away a good many of our hands. I would advise settling accounts with the month men for the year if the weather should not soften in a few days. Nine and three-quarters mile of canal have been completed so far.

The Sixth Year - 1798

This year we erected a new saw mill and a new grist mill on the Concord River. We now have two blacksmith shops, two saw mills, and two grist mills.

I had a little contretemps with some of the workmen who banded together and demanded that their wages be raised beyond $8 a month. I refused and they left.

I should note that the men are working by sunrise, stopping for breakfast and their noon meal only as long as it takes to eat them, and then quitting at sunset. In the summer in hot weather they are allowed an hour and a half break, in which case they work about twenty minutes after sunset. Twice a day the cry "Grog-o" rings out and the work stops long enough for a drink to lift up their spirits.

I was much annoyed with Joseph Snow who worked from late April for about a month and then left before we paid him to go back and work on his farm. In July he came back and promised to stay on the job with us if I gave him his back pay. I agreed,

---

Previous pages: left, Floating towpath, Billerica Mill Pond (Watercolor, c. 1822, by Jabez Ward Barton: Courtesy Billerica Historical Society); right, Floating towpath from opposite side (Watercolor, c. 1822, by Jabez Ward Barton: (from the Collection of The New-York Historical Society)

but after a few days, he left again. Of course with some of our workers coming from the farms, it is to be expected I suppose that they will leave for planting and harvesting seasons. Their family calls them home, or farm wages go up and it profits them to leave us.

On Aug.24, when the three locks on the Merrimack were finally perfected, I made the first passage up and down them, accompanied by fifteen workmen. Everything answered completely the purpose designed.

Much of our work was carried on by contractors who engaged to dig a section of the canal for a certain sum. I was sympathetic to the plight of Benjamin Dowse who contracted to dig 250 rods of the canal for us at $13.50 per rod. This was almost a mile in length. He discovered many obstructions that he could not have forseen, and lost money on the arrangement. He asked that the directors consider his case and make a further allowance to save his famnily from distress. They agreed and gave him an additional $500. I also urged upon them some kind of a present for his son who had labored hard on the job and been much exposed to cold and wet. I suggested that nothing could be more proper than clothes to warm those limbs which had suffered so much. They agreed and we bought him a full outfit, including shoes, a hat, and a muslin handkerchief all for for $22.44.

The Seventh Year - 1799

Costs were beginning to rise on the canal work. In three locks I had used one thousand tons of stone. All these stone were torn out of a ledge by severe hard labor. Because of the nature of the ledge we used little gun powder. The boating of the stone is expensive, there is constant need of more trass. After due consideration we decided that further locks should be built of wood which would be more within our means. In the future only locks near rivers would be built of stone, the rest would have to be constructed largely of wood.

The Eighth Year - 1800

The board of directors reviewed the line of the canal on August 24 and are pleased with the exertions we are making to remove the bar of earth and stones in the deep cutting near the Concord River. They have authorized me to use as many men as possible to clear the passageway here. They also ask that I finish the lock at Beard's place, so the canal can be filled to Wilmington.

The Ninth Year - 1801

In early March we let water into the canal to the west of Concord River. I went up in a boat to the head of the canal with Leonard Jarvis and found that section of the canal all clear of ice.

This year we were engaged in building the aqueduct over the Shawsheen river in Billerica. It was very difficult work. But when it was completed, water filled the canal to the first lock in Wilmington.

In October the south bank of the canal at Shawsheen broke and had to be repaired. We also launched the new boat at Billerica which is 70 feet in length. In December we got the first raft of lock timber down the canal to Jaques basin.

The Tenth Year - 1802

In January we had water in the canal down to the gravel pits in the Hastings land at Wilmington. In April I was busy in laying out the aqueduct to go over the Aberjona river in Woburn [Winchester]. The same month a raft and pleasure boat made it down the canal to my house from the Merrimack. In May I laid out the Gardners lock pits.

I have received a request from Peter C. Brooks, who has sold us at cost the eighty foot wide strip of land through his estate that we will be using in Medford for the canal. He asks that we build him one convenient bridge across the canal, and to support the fences all along the pathways of the canal to prevent the inroads of his neighbor's cattle. He makes this a condition of his sale to us. He also asks for two culverts under the canal. We will of course oblige him.

In April a raft, loaded with 600 tons of timber, board, and planks, came sixteen miles down the canal as far as Woburn

The workmen during May have exerted themselves of late and have with the greatest cheerfulness gone into the water many times, often times up to their armpits, and continued wet for whole days together. I determined to ask the directors if I can promise them some kind of treat for such behavior. Perhaps on our national day of July 4 I could give them liberty to suspend work for part of the day so they might enjoy it. I think this would have a good effect in stimulating them to further exertions.

By this summer we were able to establish regular passenger service on the canal for travellers between Billerica and Chelmsford. In two hours, for twenty-five cents, the "Great Boat," which had been christened the *George Washington* made the trip daily. Slowly we began to bring in some revenue to the proprietors. Our two gristmills also brought in money. The two sawmills principally provided timber for the canal.

On July 4th, in honor of our nation's birth, we filled the *Washington* barge with 126 ladies and gentlemen and took them up the canal from Medford to Maple Meadow.

As I summed up the work of this year for the proprietors we had completed nine locks, one aqueduct, and a number of bridges over the canal that were formed, placed, and finished. There are now 1200 tons of timber on the waters of this canal moving on towards Boston. The banks of the canal appear to be firm and the mechanism of the locks complete and easy in their operations.

By the end of this year the canal was complete from the Merrimack to the Mystic River in Medford. Our attention for the next year has to be to complete the canal between that place and the tide water in Charlestown.

The Eleventh and Last Year - 1803

In March of this year I did not attend the canal meeting in Boston. I have been so harrassed by the directors with petty demands and contradictory orders, that I have pretty much determined to quit the canal work.

I shortly received a most sympathetic and understanding letter from Judge Sullivan. He assures me that there is no distrust or discontent in the minds of the Directors with my work as an artist; that they have never had, even for a moment, a want of confidence in my attachment to the project, nor to my integrity. He beseeches me, since we are so near the end of the project, to persue the enterprise to its rightful conclusion that will bring honor and laurels to all our brows. I have determined to accede to his most sincere request.

As a result by March 10 I was out with a committee looking for land to buy for the canal from Medford to Charlestown. The next two days were spent staking out land for the canal. On the 21st I was in Charlestown staking out the canal. Late that month I went to Providence to purchase castings for the paddle gates for a canal lock.

By April I was measuring for the aqueduct over the Mystic river in Medford. We sent timber down to build it from our mill in Billerica.

In order to provide a proper terminus for the canal in Charlestown, we purchased its mill pond, dam, mills, and wharfs in August for $11,250.

As of late August Mr. Jaques has only at most 10 men working on his section of the canal. He has twenty others in reserve waiting for us to empty the canal so that he can proceed to clear the canal of grass and other obstructions from the Mill Pond down to Horn Pond.

Nov. 24 the directors told me they want the Malden Road lock finished as soon as possible and I was to hire as many men as required to complete the work.

Finally, the end of the great project came. At two o'clock in the morning of December 31, 1803, the water for the first time passed through the Middlesex Canal into the waters of the mill pond in Charlestown. We completed the whole work within the ten year time we had set for ourselves back in 1793, and the cost of the whole proved to be half a million dollars, which included not only the nearly thirty miles of the canal itself, but the cost of the land we purchased, the bridges, culverts, sluiceways, etc, we built, and the various mills etc. that we established.

Now one yoke of 0xen could draw on the canal eight hundred tons of timber. To bring the same amount to Boston on land would take six hundred teams of four oxen each. This is an enormous saving in labor and cost. And we have opened to the Boston market a connection by water with the extensive country up to the Merrimack river and beyond. This enterprise exceeds in magnitude any other project undertaken in the northern part of the United States and brings glory to all.

The Year 1804

A group of Medford businessmen, Benjamin, Richard, and Nathaniel Hall of Medford, had long been dissatisfied with the proprietors decision to extend the canal into Charlestown instead of ending it at Medford as originally planed. We have therefore agreed that the Middlesex Canal will build a feeder canal from the nearest place on our canal to the river. There is a growing ship building industry in Medford which can make use of the timber brought down on the canal. I am to aid them in this project.

On October 8 the Middlesex Canal Proprietors granted an indenture to the Halls giving them permission to open such a branch canal to the Mystic River. It was to have two locks, one from a basin at the junction of the branch and Middlesex canal, and the other a tide lock into the river. They would also be required not to interrupt the towing path on the Middlesex canal, but must maintain a bridge towing path where the basin joins the Middlesex sufficient for horses and oxen to pass on with a draw for the passage of boats and rafts.

The Year 1805

On February 18, although the incorporation act had not yet passed the legislature, I presented the Middlesex canal proprietors with a drawing showing that the traveling bridge I proposed to erect over the Medford Turnpike road would be four feet nine inches above the top of the Turnpike road. They agreed to this.

March 16 the act incorporating the proprietors of the Medford Branch Canal and Locks passed the legislature and I could begin actual work on this canal. It will let timber down from New Hampshire to Thatcher Magoun's new shipyards in that town.

This feeder canal will be 1320 feet long, or a quarter of a mile total. Each of the two locks will be about 75 feet long, the usual length for most of the Middlesex canal locks, and provide a lift of between seven and ten feet.

By the end of the year the branch canal was in operation.

Taming the Merrimack

The year is 1900 and I teach English at the high school in Concord, New Hampshire. My father Massena who loved his Shakespeare named me Miranda after Prospero's young and innocent daughter in The Tempest. When I was growing up in the 1860s, Abraham Lincoln was our president then, my grandfather Hosea told me and my brothers and sisters about his ride with his Pa on the old Middlesex Canal that went from Boston to our state. I really loved the story of his first ride on that canal in 1815.

Ever since I've been interested in our American canals, especially those of my home state of New Hampshire. Over the years I made a hobby of tracing as many of them as I could and have been lucky enough to ride on parts of some and to have walked many a former towpath. This winter I decided to write this account of those along the Merrimack for my nieces, nephews, and their offspring. I hope that they will enjoy it.

Question: how many falls are there on our New Hampshire Merrimack River between Massachusetts and Concord? Three? Seven? Well, if you had guessed those numbers you would have guessed wrong for the correct answer is eleven - and a "should be." They are as follows: Cromwell's Falls, Moor's Falls, Cohas Falls, Goff's Falls, Griffins Falls, Short Falls, Merrill's Falls, Amoskeag Falls, Hooksett Falls, Bow Falls and Turkey Falls. The "should be" is the Wicasee Falls at Tyngsboro which while it is just over our border and so technically in Massachusetts still blocked our Merrimack River from flowing freely to its meeting with the Middlesex Canal.

Now look at the map of New Hampshire. What do you see? Well, lots of small and middle-sized rivers which are dominated by two great rivers: the Connecticut which divides Vermont and her Green Mountains from our beautiful state and the Merrimack which is the result of the junction of the Pemigewasset and Winnipesaukee rivers at the rise of the White Mountains in the south central part of the state. It then proceeds to flow down to our border with Massachusetts and that great city of mills and canals Lowell, and eventually 110 miles from its source it reaches the Atlantic at Newburyport. Its name, which has been corrupted by the settlers from Europe, means in the local American Indian dialect "swift water."

When Loammi Baldwin and his friends decided to build their Middlesex Canal in 1793 one of the chief reasons they did so was so that our New Hampshire oaks and pines, indeed lumber of

Locks on Amoskeag canal (Courtesy Manchester, NH, City Library)

every kind, the produce such as corn, rye, and potatoes grown by our farmers, even the manure from our cows and horses, as well as the various goods and merchandise our people made, could be easily and quickly shipped to the port of Boston, and from there to - well to everywhere. To achieve this goal involved using the Merrimack but all its falls and rapids made that impossible. So dams, locks, and canals had to be constructed to get the rafts and barges around them and on their journey again.

That task fell principally to John Langdon Sullivan who was from 1808 to 1820 the superintendent of the Middlesex. He attacked the problem with all the vigor he possessed, which was a lot, and by 1815 the river was generally navigable from Lowell to Concord. A few years later the steamship *Merrimack* was able to tow three boats and their cargo, totaling 39 tons, up the canal to Concord, New Hampshire. It was even able to go eight miles beyond Concord to Sewall's Falls, and did so on June 18, 1819 with 157 passengers aboard, a band playing loudly and often, and towing two loaded barges. I wish I could have been on board the *Merrimack* that day!

Between the city of Concord and the town of Chelmsford, some fifty-three miles in length, the Merrimack had a drop of 135 feet, and so the Proprietors of the Middlesex Canal authorized the building of a series of canals. Here is what I know about them.

THE WICASEE CANAL at Tyngsboro, just about four miles from where the Middlesex Canal joins with the Merrimack, was a short canal with but one dam and lock. It was built by one hundred men and completed in 1815 at a cost of 14,000 dollars.

I found this interesting account about the canal written by Mr. Sullivan in the Concord Public Library. "A rapid for half a mile between an island and the western shore, is crossed with a dam of stone and timber, 200 yards; this raises the water above about a foot, which saved digging on the other side of the island, where the lock is placed. This side afforded a passage for high water, six rods wide. From the lock to its entrance is 1900 feet. This space was encumbered with masses of rock of every size, and with earth, estimated at 4000 square yards. The lock is placed in the middle of the stream; its side walls are 100 feet in length, connected with the shore by wing-walls, each about 50 feet. The wing-walls are faced with plank driven into the bottom and extending into the shore. The walls having no support, were necessarily thick, to sustain the pressure of the lock, and the shock of freshets. They are 12 feet high, and average 8 feet thick; contain 1200 perches. The stone was split out large, and drawn half a mile, loaded for the most part on to a boat with a crane and windlass, and thence laid. The foundation was difficult, the bottom was encumbered with stones, the water from 2 to 7 feet deep, and not being clear, the work of deepening, filling up, and laying the walls under water, was done by feeling, diving, &c."

Question: Do any of you know what "1200 perches" are? If not, look it up in the dictionary at your public library.

CROMWELL'S CANAL, the first in New Hampshire, was thirteen miles further up the river between Litchfield and Merrimack. Before the dam, lock and small canal were constructed boats attempting to navigate the rapids here were often damaged or even completely lost. It cost 9,000 dollars to build the dam and its 600 perches of stone came from within a mile of the site. It extended about 120 rods in the river on the westerly side; its lock raised the boats six feet and then they went along the canal to return to the river above the falls. The canal was fully operational by 1815.

I found this interesting account in the diary of a local man there, John Bowers. He is probably remembering the canal about

Colonel Blodget

1850. "The river falls thirty feet in about half a mile here at Cromwell's Falls, down by our meadow land and when I was a little boy, the old locks there were kept up and there was a little house where the lock tender lived."

UNION LOCKS AND CANALS. In 1808 the New Hampshire legislature gave a charter to the "proprietors of the Union Locks and Canal" which allowed them to build dams and locks on the Merrimack from Reed's Ferry which was between the towns of Litchfield and Merrimack up to the Amoskeag Falls at Manchester. The falls here were six in number: Moor's, Cohas, Goff's, Griffins, Short, and Merrill's and to bypass them the company erected for a stretch of nine miles seven locks and six dams. The hard work was finished by 1813 and the cost was 56,772 dollars.

In 1813 the legislature voted to allow the company to run a Lottery to raise 20,000 dollars to help it meet the expenses of construction provided that Massachusetts allowed the sale of tickets in their state. Massachusetts agreed but in the end the Lottery was a failure. Instead of raising money it saddled the company with a debt exceeding 5,000 dollars.

The locks on this canal followed a similar pattern although special conditions at the different localities in which they were built obviously affected their construction. Each fall required but a single lock except for Moor's which needed two because of the extensive nature of the falls and the fact that the water was shallow. The first raised a boat four feet, the second six feet. The dams were made of timber, stone, and plank. I learned from studying the records of the company that making these locks and dams proved to be difficult due to the height of the river banks and also often dangerous because spring freshets were a common occurrence.

I found this interesting account of a vacation trip taken by boat by Pliny Steele Boyd in 1879 which involved passage through the old Union Canal and its falls. "After breakfast we girded ourselves for action; and found an hour's perilous work in ascending Moore's [sic] falls, whose music had mingled with the roar of thunder during the night. We made the passage of the falls through the old canal, finding but three points of special danger and difficulty. By rowing, towing, lifting, and carrying, we gained the victory, and were ready for further endeavor...The canals that had once been a help to navigation were in such dilapidated condition as to be attractive chiefly as ruins. Large stones once forming symmetrical walls, were tumbled in delightful confusion, stained with age, and grown over with vines and bushes...The old locks were but piles of rocks in our way. A little willow grove just below the railroad bridge at Goff's Falls invited us to lunch that noon."

AMOSKEAG CANAL began as Blodget's Canal. In many ways these falls with their drop of 45 feet were the greatest challenge to navigating the Merrimack. In 1794 Judge Samuel Blodget, a well-to-do citizen of Derryfield (since 1810 part of Manchester), decided to build on his own land which was adjacent to the river a private canal which would free the river to boats and rafts. He began the needed excavating and erecting of dams.

Four years later New Hampshire gave the necessary public permission for him to build his private canal around the Amoskeag Falls; he was also given the right to collect tolls from the boats that were to use his canal. Things, however, did not sail smoothly for the Judge and he soon was up to his ears in debts. So New Hampshire generously gave him additional time to accomplish his goals and to help him financially voted him the right to conduct a lottery.

Well, things still did not improve for Samuel Blodget and the records indicate that he had to get from New Hampshire several time extensions and the right to hold several additional lotteries. Even Massachusetts granted him that right. None raised as much money as was needed but finally the canal was completed in 1807. But this was the second time it had been finished.

The first occasion was in 1798 when before an eager and enthusiastic crowd the Honorable Judge Blodget ordered that the gates to the lock be opened. When they were the water rushed in so suddenly that its force pushed the structure of the lock up and up. The result was a major disaster and all the Judge could do was to watch his hopes swirl madly down stream. The next year a spring freshet finished the job.

Faced with this situation, Blodget turned to his friend Loammi Baldwin who came to his aid for the Middlesex Canal needed to have the falls bypassed. Repairs were made, additional work undertaken, and in May of 1807 the mile long canal and its nine locks and several dams became a working reality. The total cost of its construction was in the neighborhood of 60,000 dollars.

Judge Blodget lived to see his vision realized. Aged 84, with bare head, he drove in a high two-wheeled gig through a line of his neighbors and local farmers to the top of the canal and boarded a raft appropriately decorated for the wonderful event. The gates were open and this time the water entering the lock behaved itself, and the raft, the Judge, and other dignitaries, sailed down past the impressive Amoskeag Falls to the applause and cheers of the gathered crowd.

On June 26, 1815 the name of the canal was changed from Blodget's to Amoskeag. A year later Mr. Sullivan reported to the Middlesex Canal Proprietors: "Amoskeag canal is the greatest work of the kind on this navigation."

Boat entering Amoskeag canal
(Courtesy Manchester (N.H.) Historic Association)

HOOKSETT CANAL is roughly eight miles above the Amoskeag Falls in the town of Dunbarton. It was not until 1822 that its name became Hooksett. The falls drop here 16 feet; in their center is a high rock. It was in 1794 that New Hampshire incorporated Robert McGregor and William Duncan as the "Proprietors of Isle of Hooksett Canal" and gave them four years to build their canal. Four years does seem like a long time but in this case it was not long enough. The four became another two, then another two, then a one and another one. In the end the canal was not completed until either 1812 or 1813, the records are not clear.

The work required not only hauling in stone over the river but digging the first lock deep into the river bottom through rocky

View of side lock at Cromwell's Falls as it exists today (Photo: Courtesy Charles Mower)

soil. Also it proved necessary to make the guard lock extra strong. In addition, the Proprietors had to purchase a dam and mills already on the site. The total cost for the three locks and digging of the canal was 15,000 dollars.

Mr. Sullivan reported to the Proprietors of the Middlesex in 1811 after the first two locks were ready that the canal had "progressed to great forwardness. It has two Locks. The first is placed in the river below the falls and the second, immediately adjoining it; they will together raise nineteen feet perpendicularly, or to a level of the river above the Falls in any state of the water at which it is navigable. To connect the second Lock with the Mills and Mill-Dam, required a high and strong wall, which is faced with plank and made water-tight. The Mill Dam is built of Timber, which being always wet, will not decay. It runs parallel to the shore for about two hundred and fifty feet till it reaches an island of rock. The Guard Gates are built between this island and the shore, supported by stone abutments of sufficient height and strength to resist the freshets of the river."

BOW CANAL, seven miles up river in the town of the same name went around Garven's Falls, the next to last falls on the Merrimack concerned with the Middlesex Canal. Built in 1812 at a cost of 21,000 dollars, its length was about half a mile and it had one dam and four locks one of which was a guard lock. The drop at Garven's Falls was 25 feet and that at Turkey Falls about a mile away, the last falls which needed to be conquered, was 5 feet. Fortunately, the dam that was constructed at Garven's raised the water level enough so that it permitted boats to flow over the latter falls as well. Once the work was finished on the Bow Canal it meant that from then on boats could go from Boston to Concord. An idea and dream had become reality. And the total cost of all this construction came to about $176,000.

At one time some of the folks connected with opening the river to traffic from here to Boston, and also the gentlemen running the Middlesex Canal, thought it might be possible to extend their enterprise clear through to Vermont and Canada. Mr. Sullivan in 1810 explained this hope: "The river Merrimack at Boscawen and Salisbury, where the three great turnpike roads to Vermont and Canada diverge, is but 40 miles from the Connecticut. Therefore that part of Vermont lying east of the mountains, and all the western part of New-Hampshire, will have Boston for its nearest and most accessible sea port."

From that point the plan was to build a canal from the Connecticut to Lake Champlain from which the St. Lawrence could be reached and thence trade could be established with Montreal and the Maritime Provinces. It certainly was a great idea but I cannot help but wonder what would have happened once the railroads had come into popular use which would probably have been about the time that the series of canals were finished.

The little settlement of Bow, by the way, is notable not just for the canal but also as the birthplace of Mary Baker Eddy, the founder of the Christian Science Church.

You might be wondering just how the boats got down and then up the river and its series of canals. In 1886 our New Hampshire General George Stark explained in great detail in his article on the canals for the *Granite Monthly* just how this was accomplished. "In going down the river between canals the usual mode of propulsion was by the use of the scull-oars. The bow-men took position close to either side of the boat, facing the bow and about six feet from it, and each worked his oar against a thole-pin placed in the opposite gunwale, the oar handles crossing, so that they were necessarily worked simultaneously. The skipper also had his oar, which he worked in a similar manner when his attention was not wholly taken up in steering." Going down river the cur-

rent made the work easier, and if a wind was blowing the men could put up a sail.

The return trip was more difficult because it had to be made against the current and so poling was almost always necessary. "To propel the boat by poling, a bow-man stood on either side of the bow, with his face towards the stern, and thrusting the pike end of his pole down beside the boat in a slanting direction towards the stern until it struck the bottom of the river, he placed his shoulder against the top of the pole, and, with his feet firmly braced against the cross-timbers in the bottom of the boat, he

The rock known as "Old Hildreth"—if this was covered by water, the boatmen need not use the bypass canals to travel down the Merrimack. Named after a Lowell businessman. Today on Merrimack Street in Lowell one can still see a building named after him. (Photo: Courtesy Charles Mower)

exerted the strength of his body and legs to push the boat forward. As it moved, he stepped along the bottom of the boat still bracing his shoulder firmly against the pole until he walked in this manner to the mast-board,—or, rather, until the movement of the boat had brought the mast-board to him. He then turned round and walked to the bow, trailing his pole in the water, thrust it again to the bottom of the river, and repeated the pushing movement." Normally it took about seven to ten days to make the trip down and back. This remained the chief mode of transporting goods to Boston until the advent of the railroad.

So that's the story of how the Merrimack River was tamed to allow boats, barges, rafts, and other vessels to travel between Concord and Boston. A new age had begun for our state of New Hampshire. Quickly, easily, and with profit, the produce and goods of our hard-working and industrious people could now reach a very large marketplace. The common effort of many individuals from that of the Proprietors to those who did the digging and from those who hauled the stone for the walls of the locks to those who supervised the engineering feats made the originating idea come to pass. If I was not alive to see all this, my grandfather through his tales made them ever vivid for me. I hope I have done the same for you.

Postscript by your Cousin Ann, July 4, 1996.
Hi Cozs. Just as our great-great (have I got enuff greats?) Aunt Miranda did, last summer Bill and I visited each of the falls and canals, or the remains of them, that she described in the account she wrote for her nieces and nephews in 1900. It was brilliant! Here's what we found.

There's very little to see at Tyngsboro now because the river is higher today than it was originally due to the Pawtucket Dam although one can still find a bit of the old canal in the stream on the eastern side of the island. And you can play a game of golf on the island too as Bill did for its now the home of the Tyngsboro Country Club. The canal and lock at Cromwell's Falls is in pretty good shape, however, and is next to an Anheuser-Busch plant. Yup, you guessed it; that's exactly what Bill did. Even I had one.

If you stand on the Boston & Maine tracks just above Reed's Ferry you can still see some signs of how the canal looked in the old days at Moor's Falls and you can also find traces of it at Cohas, Goff's, Griffins, and Short Falls. Further on from the Granite Street bridge you can see how it was at Merrill's Falls.

In Manchester, virtually nothing remains of the old Blodget canal. This canal was modified and used for power purposes for the mills and renamed the Amoskeag canal. Today, if you drive along Canal Street you will be driving where the boats once went An old stone wall can be seen which looks like a foundation. This is part of the old canal.

Finally, a bit of the canal as it was at Hooksett is still visible if one looks carefully while the upper section of the Bow canal is easily identified. The rest of it was long ago obliterated. If you have some time on a nice sunny summer's day, and you like canals, this makes a good outing.

Sketches by A. E. Herrick, 1886.
Old Residents' Historical Association *Publications, III*

How the Canal Worked

Caleb Eddy, the 51 year old Agent and Superintendent of the Middlesex Canal, was sitting at his desk at the small two-story Canal Office in Charlestown, quill in hand. He didn't really like preparing these annual reports for the directors but it was a part of his job. The first had been in 1825 and this report for 1835 would be his tenth. He wondered if these were as dull reading for the directors as it had been for him in drafting them.

Sighing, he glanced out of his open window at the Mill pond with its rafts, floating logs, and the *Governor Sullivan* preparing to set off for Horn Pond. The scene was certainly lively and, as always, he enjoyed the confusion and noise associated with Landing No. 1 on the east side of Mill pond. Maybe that's it, he thought. Maybe I should share with the directors the hustle and bustle, the everyday excitement and problems connected with running the canal. He nodded. That was it. He would make a special inspection of the canal from Boston to Lowell and write it up as his annual report. Caleb sat back in his chair and let a smile take possession of his broad kindly face.

Men scything grass in canal

The morning was cloudless, cool, and serene. Eddy had arisen with the sun and was now walking to the Canal Office. This was the day he was going to take one of the canal's laboring boats and travel up to Lowell to get a first-hand view of daily operations for the report he was planning to write for the directors.

He was in an extremely good mood and passing one of the city's horse-wagons collecting refuse brought to mind the two terms he had served on the Board of Aldermen just after Boston formally become a city in 1822. That had been a busy period in his life and he had enjoyed getting to know and working with Mayor Quincy especially relating to improving street cleaning and planning the new market at Fanueil Hall (soon to be called the Quincy Market after the mayor). But all that was just before he had been hired as superintendent of the Middlesex Canal to replace James Fowle Baldwin, one of the engineering sons of Loammi Baldwin. Several people had been interested in the job but when Mr. Eddy had received Mayor Quincy's strong recommendation for the position that had given him the edge over the other candidates. He smiled and decided that perhaps the demands of being an alderman had been worth the effort after all.

At the Canal Office he first took care of a couple of matters left unfinished from the day before, for Caleb Eddy was a practical man and was well known for his business skills. After all he had been a merchant and had run a store with his friend Bemis in Boston for seventeen years. He should know something about the business world. Having cleared his desk, he walked into the Collector's Office run by his colleague, Richard Frothingham, to examine some of the recent passports.

Caleb Eddy

Passports were required of all craft operating on the canal. A passport gave the date of travel, the craft's number (and all boats on the canal had to have a number), the owner's name, and the articles transported. They were obtained from the lock keeper where each boat commenced its journey and needed to be signed by the keeper of every lock passed through. When the boat arrived at its final destination the owner had to turn over his passport to the Collector at the Landing who calculated the toll due, collected that amount, and then gave instructions for the unloading of the boat. Caleb always found it instructive to review a group of them for it gave him a pretty clear idea of how businesses and individuals were using the canal and it also gave him a sense of the usefulness of the whole enterprise.

Satisfied that the passports were being filled out properly and that the Collectors were charging the appropriate tolls, Caleb Eddy left the Canal Office and strolled about the Landing. The Canal maintained nine of them from Boston to Lowell and they were crucial to its effectiveness. Each landing had its own basin, wharf, and toll collector. The locks were cared for and opened and shut by their own tenders who also had to inspect the passport and attend to other clerical duties. Since he always kept a sharp eye on the maintenance needs at the Charlestown landing he decided he did not have to inspect it on this trip, so he went down to the laboring boat, stepped aboard, greeted its captain and crew, and with a blast on the large tin horn, a piece of equipment standard to every craft, they shoved off.

There were two items uppermost in Eddy's mind on this first leg of the voyage. He wanted to see and talk with the men working on a stretch of the high embankment beyond the Ox-Bow Bend in Wilmington. This had sunk during the spring thaw and he wanted to check out a couple of reports of leaks caused by muskrats and minks. Fortunately for the canal, when this happened one of the nearby farmers or even just a neighbor in the area who had been walking along the tow path and noticed the leak would report the matter to one of the lock tenders who passed the information along to the Agent. It was vital to mend such repairs as soon as possible just as it was important to respond to damage done wantonly and maliciously by humans.

As they got started Caleb's attention was caught by the double tidal gates which opened either way to let boats from the Mill pond into the Charles River. These were fifteen feet wide and when opening or shut resulted in a lot of water being drained from the pond. Just too much water he had concluded three years ago and had strongly recommended to the Proprietors that the width be reduced by five inches but that had not yet been done.

The horse towing their laboring boat was a beautiful golden color and altogether a magnificent creature whose name appropriately enough was Goldie. Eddy had a deep fondness for horses and any ill treatment of them by a tow hand meant instant loss of his job. Even so towing was very hard on a horse and some suffered greatly from skin sores under their collars due to friction and irritation from the tow line. When that happened they would need special care for a week or ten days before they could be used again. Suddenly Caleb chuckled. Perhaps they should rub a bit of Medford Rum on those sores, he thought. It was certainly a fiery stimulant!

The boat slowed near the Mystic Lakes for it was along here that the first leak caused by muskrats had been reported. Sure enough there it was and not just one. The damage was not so great that canal traffic had to be halted to have it repaired immediately. It probably could wait until the water was drawn down for winter but obviously the bank watch needed to attend to it and plug it tightly with straw. At times the muskrat problem was so serious that the canal offered a bounty on them and in 1809, long before his days as Agent, the Treasurer had to paid $91.01

for the 265 minks and muskrats that been caught by those living along the banks of the Middlesex that year.

It was also when the water was drawn down in the spring, done by opening the gates into the Concord and Merrimack and the sluices to the various streams and brooks, that not only animal damage to the banks was repaired but also everything else from paddle gates and locks, sluice ways and drains, aqueducts and stone work. It was certainly one of the busiest times for the staff of the canal.

It was not long after they had passed Col. Baldwin's place that they came to where the embankment was being rebuilt beyond the Ox-Bend and the Maple Meadow and its brook. The two men who had been assigned the task, Daniel Wilson and Israel Colson from North Billerica, put down their tools when they saw the laboring boat with their boss approaching. This year Wilson was

Passport (Photo: Mogan Library, Lowell)

59

RATE OF TOLL

ON THE

MIDDLESEX CANAL......UNTIL FURTHER NOTICE.

APRIL 4, 1808.

ON all articles (excepting thoſe which follow) by weight at 6¼ cents a ton,	Dolls. Cts.
each and every mile, the whole diſtance being 27 miles	1,68¾
Timber { Oak—per mile, 6¼ cents a ton	1,68¾
Timber { Pine—per mile, 4 cents	1,08
Pine Boards } 6¼ cents	
Pine Plank, reduced to board meaſure } 6¼ cents	1,68¾
Clapboards—4 cents a thouſand	1,08
do. freight in the Proprietors' Boats—64 cents a thouſand	
Shingles—1 cent a thouſand	
Oak Plank, 2½ inch—6¼ cents for 600 feet board meaſure	1,68¾
Aſh Plank, 2½ inch—6¼ cents for 700 feet board meaſure	1,68¾
Staves, Barrel—6 cents per thouſand	1,62
do. Hogſhead—12 cents	3,24
do. Pipe—18 cents	4,86
do. Butt—25 cents	6,75
Hoops, Hogſhead—8 cents per thouſand	2,16
do. Barrel—4 cents	1,08
do. Half-Barrel—3 cents	,81
Hoop-Poles, Hogſhead- -18 cents per thouſand	4,80
do. Barrel—9 cents	2,40
Shucks, 40 to be rated as one ton—6¼ cents	1,68¾
do. with heads, 40 to be rated as one and an half ton, or 27 a ton—6¼ cents	1,68¾
Hogſheads, empty, 20 to be rated as a ton, or at 8¼ cents each	1,68¾
Barrels, empty, 50 to a ton	1,68¾
Half-Barrels, empty, 80 to a ton	1,68¾
Corn / Rye } 40 buſhels to a ton, or 4 cents, 2 milles a buſhel	1,68¾
Oats, 80 buſhels to a ton, or 2 cents, 1 mille a buſhel	1,68¾
Rock Salt, 28 buſhels to a ton	
Coarſe Salt, 30 buſhels to a ton	
Coarſe Fine Salt, 34 buſhels to a ton	
Fine Salt, 40 buſhels to a ton	
Oars, for 1000 feet—4 cents a mile	
Wood and Bark per cord, whole diſtance 27 miles, or from above Concord River	1,17
to Medford, 22 miles	1,00
ditto from between Hopkins's Lock and Concord River,	
to Medford, 19 miles	,90
to Charleſtown, 22 miles	1,00
ditto from between Wilmington Lock and Hopkins's Lock	
to Medford, 14 miles	,65
to Charleſtown, 17 miles	,75
ditto from between Horn-Pond Lock and Wilmington Lock,	
to Medford, 12 miles	,60
to Charleſtown, 15 miles	,70
ditto from between Medford-Pond Lock and Horn-Pond Lock,	
to Medford, 7 miles	,40
to Charleſtown, 10	,50

List of tolls

serving as a representative from Billerica to the Great and General Court and Colson had plans to run for the selectman's office in Wilmington.

This was not the first time that they had trouble here with the embankment sinking. Actually it was a long term problem for the canal because for more than half of its length it had banks artificially raised above the natural level of the ground. When the ice of winter relaxed its grip on the earth each spring it resulted in numerous cases of the banks just giving way and washing into the canal bed or of making the tow path level with the water level in the canal. So they had to be built up again which was the task this day of Wilson and Colson who were frequently employed to repair the canal.

Eddy talked over the situation with them, inspected their work which was excellent as usual. He told them about the other report he had of muskrat activities. They told him that they had noticed the leaks on their way from Billerica and had repaired them. After a bit of pleasantries about their family, the two men went back to their job and Eddy ordered the laboring boat to continue on. He felt relieved that the situation here was not worse.

Goldie continued plodding steadily along the tow path, drawing the laboring boat nearer and nearer to Landing No. 7 at Billerica Mills. It certainly was a most pleasant day and Caleb permitted himself to relax for a moment and to enjoy just being a passenger. His mind drifted back to his morning thoughts about the Boston days when he had served as one of the city's Aldermen. And don't forget, he reminded himself, you also ran for the position of mayor in 1828. It was to replace his friend Josiah Quincy. He had been put up by the Jeffersonian Republicans but after two ballots neither he or his opponent had the necessary majority and so the famous Senator Harrison Gray Otis had entered the contest and won.

Suddenly Caleb's attention was caught by one of the handsome oaks the repair boat was passing. Oaks, he thought, were admirable trees and then he wondered what he would have been doing today if he had been elected for certainly he would have had to resign as the canal Agent.

Since they had travel some 22 miles since leaving the Mill pond at seven A. M., it was past Caleb's dinner time so when they docked at the Landing he announced his intentions of getting a bite at the nearby Farmer's Tavern. Before he did so, however, he wanted to inspect the dam. It had originally been built of wood and it was discovered that wood just could not withstand the constant water pressure or take the wear and tear of the seasons. One of his first projects was to have it replaced by a stone dam. Now he was involved in gradually having all the perishable wooden locks of the canal also rebuilt of stone.

After a careful survey he decided that the dam was in pretty good shape although it would need pointing next spring before the water was let back into the canal. In fact every April while the water was out all the gates, the stone work, the aqueducts, and the canal banks were repaired. Sometimes staging was needed for the work of pointing. But it was all part of the Agent's duties and Caleb did not mind.

At Farmer's he enjoyed a bounteous dinner—a boiled leg of mutton, new potatoes, pease, turnips—and some fine strong Medford Rum. Medford Rum was a favorite drink on the canal and usually every skipper had a gallon jug under the steering sweep at the stern of the boat, and it was also available at the many taverns along the route of the canal where it was often mixed with molasses.

As he ate he reminisced about how his kids and others loved it when the canal was drawn off because they could clamber down to the muddy bottom and capture the eels, suckers, chubs, and hornpout that had been stranded as the water rushed out. The braver lads also like to crawl down the paddle culvert of one lock and follow the gloomy stone and brick subterranean conduit to the next one. When his meal was finished, and he had a little more Medford Rum, Caleb felt quite restored to his tasks and walking back to the Landing he was smiling, and smiled even more when he spotted Sam Hadley Sr. and his young son Sam Jr. down from Middlesex Village as arranged.

Sam had worked for the canal for many years and for some time had the job of running the canal operations at its terminus in the Village. His son was a vigorous four year old and reminded Caleb just a bit of his own son Albert who was three. He and his wife Caroline had three living children. Sadly three others had died within a few years of their birth.

Eddy nodded at the younger man and said to his son, "When you get a bit older boy we'll give you a job on the canal." The boy gave a toothy grin. And in fact when he was a teenager he did work odd jobs for the canal and remembered those days in his old age long after his retirement from the judicial bench with much pleasure. Indeed he not only worked on it he had fished it, swam it, skated it, floated toy boats on it, almost drowned within it, and knew every captain and boatman who used it.

As they boarded the laboring boat Caleb asked, "Are they scything?" He was referring to the two Irish Guyton brothers who kept the canal clear of water-grass. Before leaving Charlestown he had heard that this stretch of five miles between North Billerica and the Village was overrun with vegetation and proving troublesome for the boats. So he had asked Sam to have it taken care of and also to meet him at the Mills.

"We'll being seeing them shortly," Sam replied.

Young Sam in the bow was soon shouting, "There they are, there they are." Two heads were soon visible in the water. The men were moving slowly in the canal water, following its bed,

BOUNTY

ON

Musquashes and Mink,

TAKEN ON THE

Middlesex Canal.

IF within two rods of the Canal, 50 cents a head ; quarter of a mile, 30 cents ;. half a mile, 10 cents ; one mile, 5 cents.

Application to be made either to Mr. Cyrus Baldwin, Mr. Nathan Mears, Col. Hopkins, Mr. Isaac Johnson, Mr. Elijah Peirce, Mr. Samuel Gardner, or Mr. Joseph Church, whichever of them lives nearest the place where the animal may be taken.

If the person applied to is satisfied of the facts, his certificate or verbal declaration thereof to the subscriber will entitle the applicant to the bounty. The applicant must produce the Musquash or Mink entire, to one of the above-named persons. He may then take his skin.

J. L. SULLIVAN.

MARCH, 1809.

Bounty of Muskrats (Photo; Mogan Library, Lowell)

their backs bent as they swung their scythes much as farmers do when haying. Once cut, the grass floated to the surface in smelly clumps. Then it drifted to the locks at Middlesex Village where it was passed through into the Merrimack. It was important not to let such aquatic grass clog the lock gates.

As Eddy and Sam conversed about the canal, Sam's son rode on the bow, and the laboring boat made its slow but steady way to Middlesex Village. It glided past Baldwin's woods with its oaks and pines, gurgling brook and alders, by the cottages that the glass workers once lived in and crossed Black Brook on its wooden aqueduct. "We've got to replace that one some day," commented Caleb. For the next quarter of a mile the canal was level, peaceful, and graced by Lombardy poplars on each side. Ahead on the right was another Baldwin house encircled with elms. Then passing under the road from Nashua, they arrived at the northern terminus of the canal.

Eddy was especially keen to see its state and to learn what work might need to be done to its buildings which he had been told were not up to the high standard he always expected. Caleb Eddy had a well earned reputation for exactness and efficiency.

The laboring boat passed between two wooden wharves and tied up at the hitching posts at the storehouse on the western side of the canal. To the north was the Collector's office, then the three locks which lowered the boats into the Merrimack river, and on the left the stable for horses and oxen. Opposite that was a kind of basin used for turning boats around. The storehouse had two floors where lime, flour, salt, and other goods could be kept temporarily. It also had space for boatmen to spend the night, and a bar. Caleb took Sam there for a draught and then began his inspection of the terminus.

His concern for its condition was justified. As he went from building to building he had Sam keep a list of what needed to be repaired. The storehouse had a couple of window sills that had rotted and should be replaced, and a heavy wooden shutter on one window was only hanging in place by luck. Fortunately its two bulkheads which he had rebuilt three years ago were holding up okay. They walked around all the buildings examining their shingling and concluded that they were sound. Maintaining a canal meant that everything had to checked each year. There was more to running a canal than just keeping its bed full of water.

"Sam, we need to check the quality of the work Dan and Israel did on that planking on the tow path under the bridge by the storehouse." It had to be planked for the safety of the horses. As usual the team of Wilson and Colson had done a fine job of it.

Finally they walked to the three locks and gave them a thorough inspection. These stone wonders, at least Eddy regarded them that way, were the first that the Proprietors and Directors had constructed and in many ways they remained the finest of all the locks on the Middlesex. They also investigated the condition of the very important basin which linked the canal to the river. Everything proved to be shipshape which was just the way that Caleb Eddy wanted it to be.

That night he dined with Sam and his family in their home on Middlesex Street, accepted their hospitality of a spare bed, rose early the next morning, and after a delicious breakfast, returned to Landing No. 1 on the laboring boat.

The very next morning, for Caleb Eddy was not a gentleman who put off what had to be done, saw him in his office at his desk quill in hand writing. "Your Agent, pursuant to the intentions of the Board, having visited and examined the Middlesex Canal, from Boston to Lowell, submits this annual report concerning its conditions and affairs for the year 1835." Caleb looked up for a moment, glanced at Landing No. 1 busy with its daily routine, chuckled, and then went back to his writing.

Dam at Mill pond in North Billerica (Photo: Thomas Dahill)

Middlesex Village (Lowell)　　　　　　　　　　Chelmsford

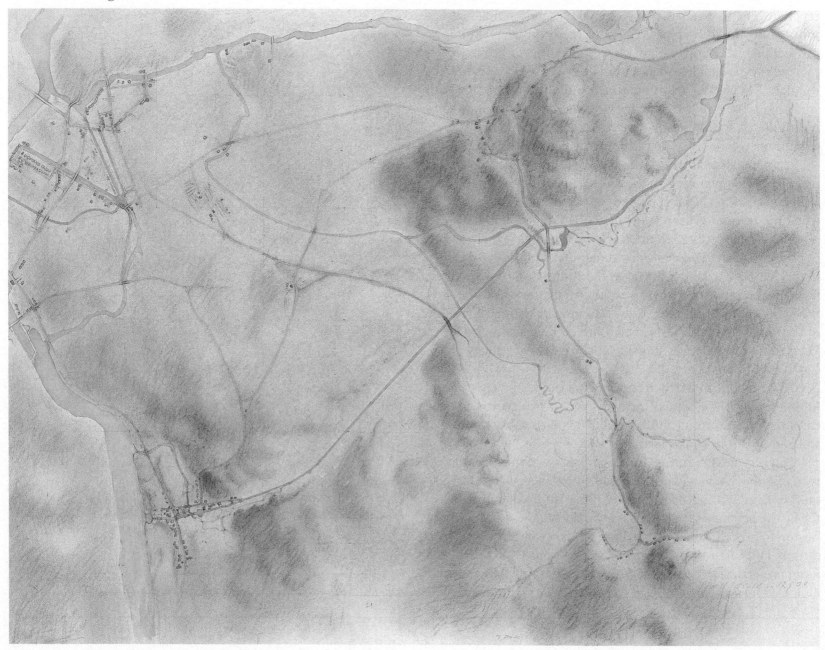

Basin Locks #18, 19, 20 Black Brook Aqueduct #8　　　　　　　River Meadow Aqueduct #7

Overview

This chapter is based on a survey of the Middlesex Canal that was ordered in 1829. George R. Baldwin, son of the late Loammi Baldwin, made the survey. Our artist has revisualized it using the field reports of Mr. Baldwin in conjunction with contemporary maps of the area. Thus, it presents a panorama of the canal as it would have appeared in 1829. The period 1829-1835 was the peak years of the canal's operation, just before the railroad began operating and eventually outmoded it.

Billerica

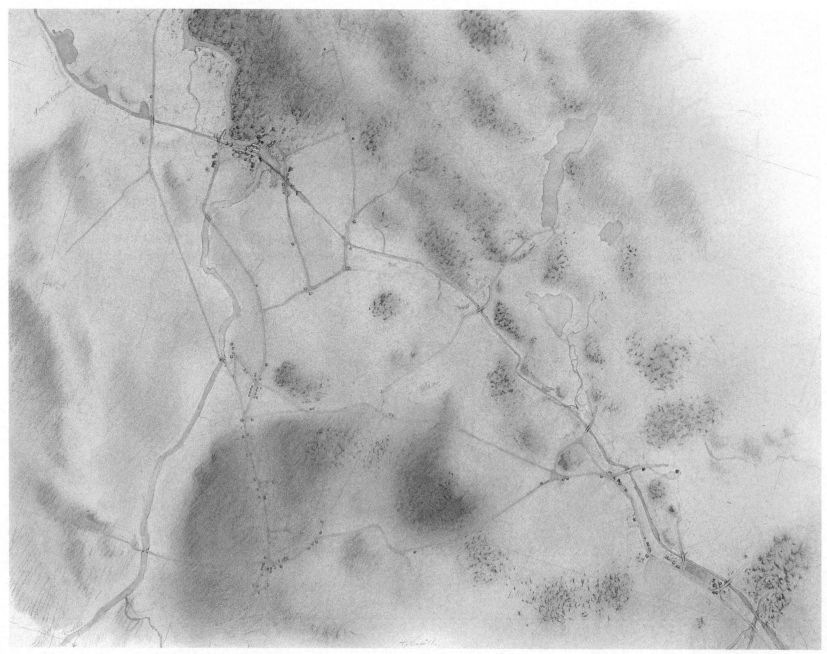

Red Lock   Millpond/Locks #17 and 16   Shawsheen Aqueduct #6

Wilmington

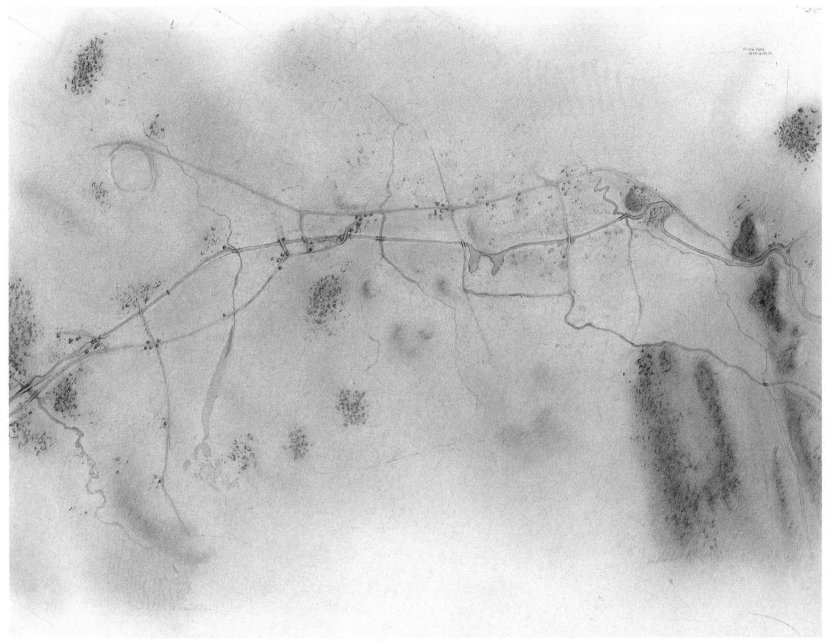

Nichols Lock #15   Gillis Lock #14, Sinking Meadow Aqueduct #5, Settle Meadow Brook Aqueduct #4,Maple Meadow Aqueduct #3

Woburn

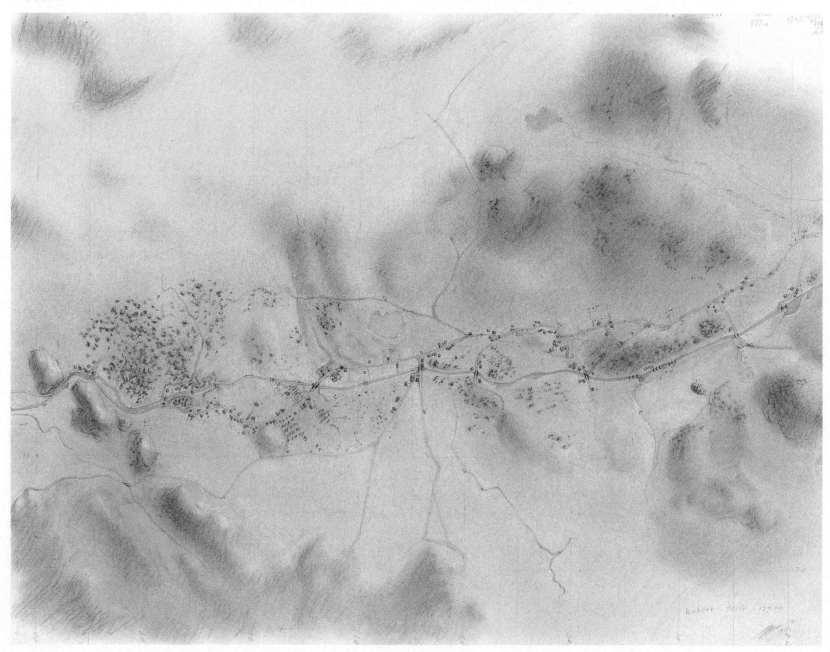

Stoddard Locks #8-#13

Winchester

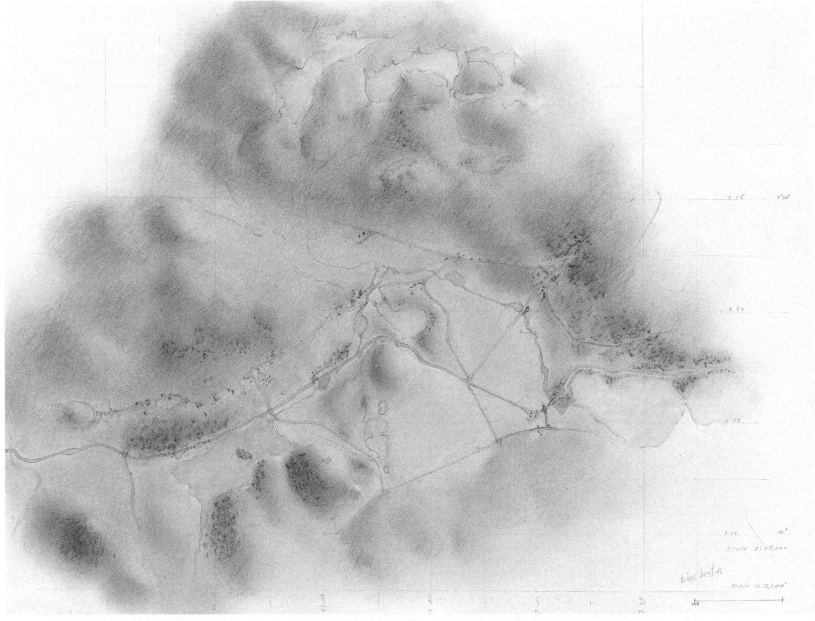

Hollis Lock #7   Gardner Locks #5 and #6   Symmes River Aqueduct #2

Medford

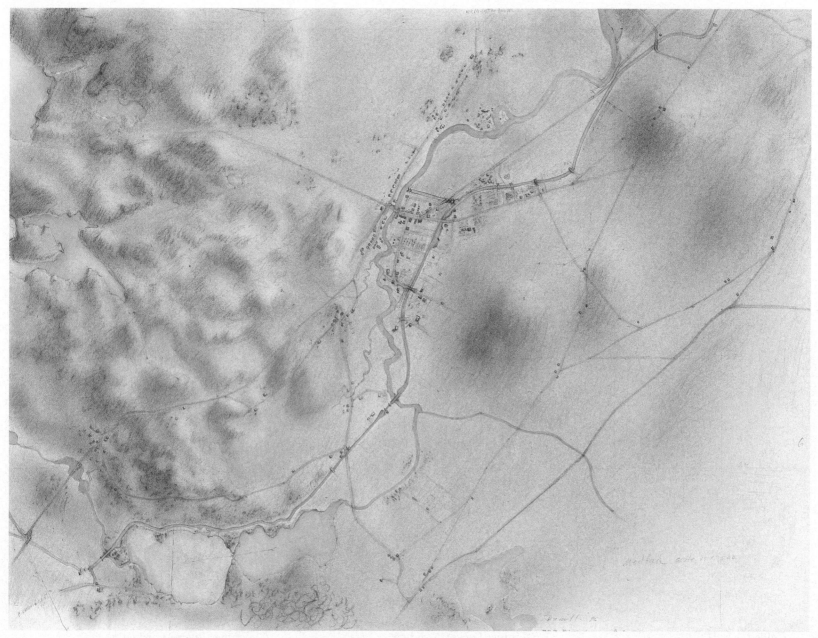

Gilson's Lock #4   Aqueduct #1   Branch Canal

Somerville   Charlestown

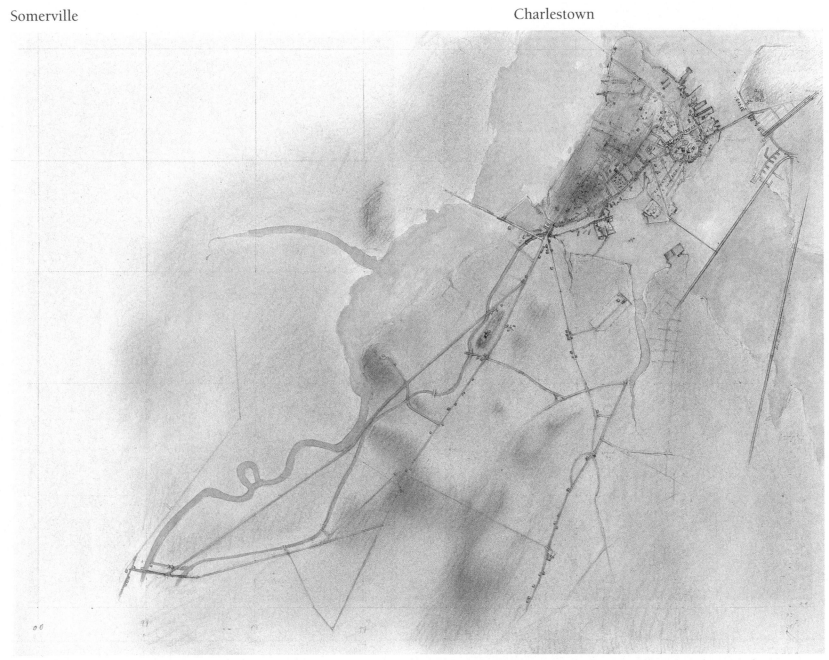

Malden Road Lock #3   Millpond Locks #2 and #1

Hadler Field, Merrimack Road, Lowell

Golf Course, Lowell

Overflight

Exactly 150 years after George Baldwin made his survey of the canal, the Middlesex Canal Commission had an aerial survey made of the canal remnants in 1979. A diligent search turned up these photographs, but they were too detailed to be used here.

Fortunately, Mr. Nolan Jones, twice president of the Middlesex Canal Association, made several flights over the route of the ca-

nal, and his photographs reproduced in this chapter cover the section of the canal from Medford to the Merrimack River. These flights were made between 1972 and 1975, We have traced the route of the canal upon his photographs, so the reader can see the canal's track over today's landscape.

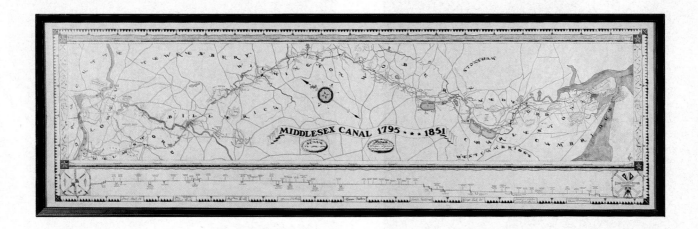

Harry J. Lasher map of the canal (Mogan Center, Lowell)

Beyond Route 3, through the Golf Course

By Route 3, Chelmsford

Canal Street, Riverneck Road, Chelmsford

Brick Kiln Road, North Billerica/Chelmsford

North from Route 3A, North Billerica/Chelmsford

Fire Station, North Billerica

North Billerica, Mill Pond

North Billerica

Billerica

Kings Corner Tavern, Billerica

Route 129, Billerica

Shawsheen Aqueduct, Wilmington Billerica Line

Wilmington Restoration

Past the Sweetheart Plant

Woburn/Wilmington Line

Past the Baldwin Mansion

By the Ramada Inn—Across Rt. 128—to Baldwin Mansion

Boy's Club, Woburn

Woburn Center

Alongside Horn Pond, Woburn

83

Thru Wildwood Cemetery, Winchester

By Sandy Beach, Winchester

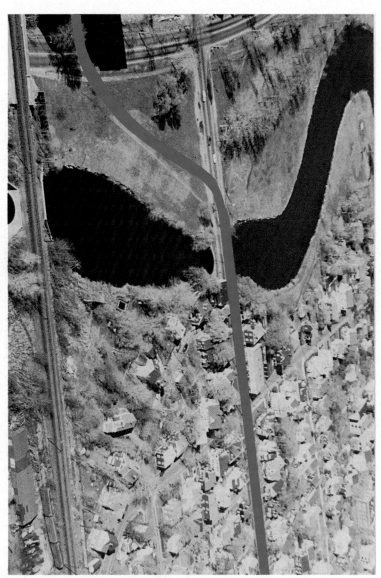

Along the Mystic Valley Parkway

Medford—Boston Avenue

Closing Down the Canal

Richard Frothingham's Account

When Caleb Eddy resigned as Agent for the canal in 1845 I was chosen to succeed him; at the time my job for the Middlesex Canal was as its Collector at the terminus in Charlestown. He and I have been friends and co-workers for years; indeed it was Mr. Eddy who persuaded me when I was 22 to leave my job at John Doggett's carpet and furniture company in Cornhill to come and work for the Middlesex. I stayed with them until the canal had to close down and then I joined the *Boston Post* as its managing editor until 1865.

I have to say that I have had a busy and fortunate life in and around Charlestown. I was its mayor for three years, that was about the time the canal was going out of business, but earlier I had served as its representative for eleven years in the General Court and was also a trustee for three years of our own Charlestown Free Schools. I am still active in my local Universalist Church and continue writing books about my town and other historical topics such as the *Siege of Boston* and the great *Battle at Bunker Hill*.

It was on January 30, 1846 that I assumed the job of Agent for the Middlesex. Unfortunately the old canal had already seen its most prosperous days and, therefore, it soon became my sad lot

Train and canal passing each other

to preside over its shutting down and closing. This is the story as best as I can put it together of how that happened.

The canal closed down for two primary reasons: the invention of the Iron Horse and because the mill owners in Lowell and New Hampshire and the wealthy business men in Boston soon understood that with railroads they would quickly realize a better return on their investments. As The Good Book might put it, in the beginning there are profits. Unfortunately for the Middlesex Canal it was never really very profitable. Strangely enough railroads appeared about the same time that our own Middlesex Canal was constructed and put into operation.

In England several inventors during the first two decades of our century were tinkering with steam power, engines, and iron rail; and the first railroad, the twenty-two mile long Stockton & Darlington line, actually began running as early as 1820. In our country serious attention was also being paid to this mode of transportation and by 1830 twenty-three miles of track had been laid. A few years later it was over a thousand miles, and by 1840 the country had three thousand miles of track. Twenty years later that figure was thirty thousand. Clearly the Middlesex Canal was doomed but of course we did not realize it at the time.

If our canal was not officially terminated until October 3, 1859, that was when the state's Supreme Judicial Court declared that the proprietors had no further canal rights, the beginning of its end was the 1829 petition to the legislature regarding a survey for a railroad between Boston and Lowell and the 1830 request filed by John F. Loring, Lemuel Pope, Issac O. Davis, Kirk Boott, Patrick T. Jackson, George W. Lyman, and Daniel Parker asking that they be allowed to incorporate as the Boston and Lowell Rail-Road Corporation. The canal proprietors immediately opposed the granting of such a charter by submitting a "Remonstrance" on February 12, 1830 with the Senate and House of Representatives.

In our statement we pointed out the generous financial investment made in the construction, maintenance, and improvement of the canal, investments made by "public-spirited men for the general good" which so far had resulted in "a heavy loss to them." Yet these same proprietors and their heirs, as well as new proprietors, many "acting for females," continued their investment because they believed "that the canal had been so long before the public, and had been so far tested by the experiment of many years, that it was a safe investment, and a permanent and an increasing one."

We also pointed out to the legislature that to our honest belief "there can never be a sufficient inducement to extend a railroad from Lowell westwardly and northwestwardly so as to make it a great avenue to and from the interior, but that its termination must always be at Lowell." Our Remonstrance questioned also the matter of passengers on trains, certainly an untried form of transportation and indicated that good service already existed by canal and coach, especially by coach, so that "passengers are now carried, at all hours, as rapidly and safely as they are any where else in the world."

Finally the proprietors asked why was there any need for a railroad to parallel the Middlesex for its "whole distance, and in many places within a few rods of it." Clearly no charter should be given but if one were the proprietors should be "indemnified for the losses which will be thereby occasioned to them."

The House of Representatives sent the Remonstrance to the Committee on Rail-ways and Canals. That committee in due time received a response to our statement from the petitioners which among other items pointed out that one of the disadvantages of the canal was that it was not in operation every month of the

Richard Frothingham

year. I have to say that was true, and it was also true that often during the winter months with their frequent storms that the stage and the teamsters had proven to be highly unreliable. The hills they have to use are often steep, often muddy, in poor repair, and, when snow-covered, dangerous. Indeed, the teamsters often quit and just walked away from their loads if it was too bad. But that is the exception, not the rule. At least that is my opinion.

Well the General Court's committee after considering all the arguments declared "that the grant of authority to build a Rail Road from Boston to Lowell would not be an infringement of the rights and privileges granted to the proprietors of the Middlesex Canal, by their charter" and that "a well constructed Rail Road between Boston and Lowell would be highly beneficial" to the public and so recommended granting the charter. In their great wisdom the General Court on June 5 concurred. They also did not vote a penny to the proprietors in compensation. I guess that we can thank our friend Daniel Webster for that vote, he who knew the canal and had enjoyed outings upon it. But Daniel was not the only one to help the railroad get built; two of Loammi Baldwin's own sons, James F. and George R., provided vital technical and engineering help during the construction of the line.

So the railroad was to be but that did not happen over night. Indeed, the Middlesex accepted the decision of the General Court for the proprietors and agent thought that while the trains might handle passengers (the canal only had about 65 passengers both ways each day for most went by stage) and light goods, the canal would continue as the chief vehicle for bulky heavy goods. With this belief, Caleb Eddy as the agent authorized the replacement of many of the old wooden locks by stone ones and indeed the building of new locks at Billerica.

Although the railroad charter was granted in 1830 it took almost five years to build the Boston and Lowell railroad and the first train with but three passengers did not make its maiden voyage from Lowell until May 27, 1835. The president of the railroad, also its agent, who was in charge of actually building the line was Patrick Tracy Jackson who knew absolutely nothing about building a railroad. Indeed he was not even an engineer and that was one of the reasons why it took so long to build the road for he first had to write to engineers in our country and in Europe for advice. He also hired Baldwin's sons to work for him. James with the assistance of a survey line drawn up in 1794 for the canal by his father was generally responsible for surveying the line while his brother George for a couple of years was responsible for gathering details on railroad building in Scotland and England. In 1836 James published his "A Plan & Profile of the Boston & Lowell Railroad." As far as I am concerned it might just as well as have been a plan and profile of our canal for it followed our route as if it were our twin brother!

The first locomotive was built in England and shipped to Lowell in bits and pieces via the Middlesex Canal as were the first granite sleepers. I guess these were the only times we made money off the railroad. The locomotive finally was put together at the Locks and Canals Machine Shops in Lowell. After that the other locomotives put into service were all built there under the direction of George W. Whistler, the father of the painter, or elsewhere in New Hampshire.

At first there was only one set of rails between Lowell and Boston; a second track was added in 1848 The latter were "T" rails on wooden ties laid in rubble; the former had been done differently and the ride was a rough one or so I was told. Eventually that was relaid on "T" rails too. The railroad did learn some lessons in its building plans from the canal. For example, it built its bridges with granite so as to avoid our problem with wood which had to be mended or replaced constantly. It took in its first years over an hour to make the rail trip of 26 miles to Boston and the fare for first class was $1.00 and that for second $.75 cents.

In 1842 when the new railroad had been operating for eight years a famous Englishman visited our country and went home and wrote about what he had done and seen. That gentleman was Charles Dickens and one of the things he did was to ride to Lowell on the new railroad. To give you a flavor of a ride on our competitor, let me share some of Mr. Dickens' observations. "There is a gentlemen's car and a ladies' car: the main distinction between is that in the first, everybody smokes; and in the second nobody does...There is a great deal of jolting, a great deal of noise, a great deal of wall, not much window, a locomotive engine, a shriek, and a bell."

The only view Mr. Dickens had of our beautiful New England countryside was this: "Mile after mile of stunted trees: some hewn down by the axe, some blown down by the wind, some half fallen and resting on their neighbours, many mere logs half hidden in the swamp, others mouldered away to spongy chips...Now you emerge for a few brief minutes on an open country, glittering with some bright lake or pool, broad as many an English river, but so small here that it scarcely has a name; now catch hasty glimpses of a distant town, with its clean white houses and their cool piazzas, its prim New England church and schoolhouse; when whir-r-r-r! almost before you have seen them, comes the same dark screen: the stunted trees, the stumps, the logs, the stagnant water." It's too bad that Mr. Dickens did not go to Lowell on the Middlesex for he would have had a much more comfortable ride and the scenery would have been far more attractive.

During the decade after the Boston and Lowell began its operations, the Middlesex attempted to carry on as usual but it was never a fair contest. If in 1836 two-thirds of the goods shipped from Lowell still went by the canal and only a third by rail, that advantage slowly but steadily shifted. Even reducing our toll charges did not help. Caleb Eddy was already thinking about the canal's future and in 1843 he published his carefully thought-out and documented proposal to stop using the canal for transportation and to utilize the waters in the canal as a source of "wholesome water" for Boston. The new company was to be incorporated as the Middlesex Water Company. The proprietors did indeed make such a petition to the General Court but the idea never became a reality.

In my first annual report as Agent to the proprietors written on February 1, 1847 after I had been in the job for a year I wrote: "The past year has been exceedingly unfortunate for the interests of the canal." That negative comment did not refer directly to the railroad; it was a reference to the frequency of freshets in 1846 and the heavy damage caused to the canal as a result; it was a reference to the low water supply available that year; it was a reference to decreasing tolls when so many repairs needed to be made; and finally it was a reference to the disastrous fire that occurred to our mills at Billerica and to the fact that we had to immediately construct there a new grist mill. These concerns in conjunction with the growing impact of the railroad is what made the situation of the canal so perilous.

My next annual report in 1848 again reflected the seriousness of the problem to be dealt with by the Middlesex Canal. I wrote then to the proprietors "There is but little hope of an increase of receipts on the River Canals, for as the Rail Roads extend into the lumber regions they will take much of the freight that now goes through them." Indeed, the Concord and Nashua Railroad which had been in service since 1842 was proving to be a prosperous operation and the Nashua and Lowell road was also doing well. To further doom the Middlesex it lost the lucrative business of transporting brick to Lowell which meant that the Union Canals as a result had very little income. At this time the Middlesex Canal's chief income was from lumber. Any hope we might have had left disappeared in 1849 when Boston diverted for its own needs water from Long Pond, the chief source of water for the Concord River and the canal which made the canal's water level often unreliable. Caleb Eddy approached the city for compensation for their action but none was given.

In what was really my final written annual report, that of 1850, it was my sad duty to remind the Directors "that the time has come to take some decisive measures with regard to the canal." In support of my statement I further reminded them that the public and our former business firms have just about ceased their use of "the whole line of canals as a means of transportation and that the point has been reached when the tolls on them will not indemnify the expense of the necessary repairs." The railroads, I declared, have "made the canals comparatively speaking useless to the public."

Finally the Directors acted. Caleb Eddy was assigned the task of drawing up a list of all the real estate held by the corporation and also of being sure that we had good title to the land. The shares in the Hooksett, Bow, and Union canals were sold; repairs to the canal were no longer authorized and so in time many of the bridges were in such bad shape that they had to be taken down. Eventually 130,000 dollars was realized from the sale of the canal's property. The last boat - it carried stone and pinewood - to travel the entire length of the canal did so on November 25, 1851. In 1852 the Directors formerly asked the Massachusetts Supreme Court for permission to close down. But death for the canal as so often happens to men and women came slowly and it was not until October 3, 1859 that the Court agreed. On April 4th the next year the Great and General Court took away from the proprietors of the Middlesex Canal all the privileges it had granted

them in 1793. And of June 4, 1860 it ordered that all the papers and records of the Middlesex Canal Company should be turned over to the Clerk of Court of Middlesex County, thus preserving them for future historians.

I should note that over the life of the canal there had been 100 assessments per share of stock amounting to $740. Because of constant repairs and improvements, we were not able to pay dividends until 1819. The total amount paid back in dividends was $559.50, a difference of $180.50. But since the assessments were paid over 23 years one should add in the interest on that money. The canal records showed simple interest at 6% as normal. That increases the cost of each share by $705.25, making the total cost of the share equal $1,445.25. That makes a loss to shareholders of $885.75.

What can one say of the generous individuals who held these shares? For they persisted in supporting this canal, not for their own financial benefit, but because of their public spirit and sense of responsibility in bringing to their community an enterprise of benefit to that community.

During the years of operation of the canal the total amount received in tolls was $868,800, excluding three years for which there was no data. The best year for tolls was in 1833, when $45,500 was received. But from 1843 onwards tolls dropped precipitously until in 1851, the last year of operation we received only $1,200. The great enterprise had reached its conclusion. The incredible ditch was incredible no more.

Some months after the canal had closed its operations, I was reading quite by chance a copy of the latest issue of Ballou's *Pictorial Drawing Room Companion* and discovered an article on the "old" canal. I read it with deep interest and enjoyment and it seems to me the right note on which to conclude my story and so I share it with you. "The Middlesex Canal has `gin eout'—`snaked out' would be a more appropriate expression. Where late a tranquil water course reflected in its polished mirror the green banks, the over-arching foliage, the light bridges, the rustic farm-houses, all the magical incidents of summer scenery; or, in winter, a bright serpentine belt of steel sustained a thousand gay forms of skaters, skimming along with the rapidity of swallows, there is only a dull gravelly or sandy furrow, like the dry moat of some abandoned fortress of the olden time. The Moorish arch on the Brooks estate, at Medford, no longer sees its inverted counterpart below. The useless locks stand gray and dry at intervals along the route. The good old Middlesex Canal, the gigantic enterprise of its day, that respectable line of communication between Boston and Lowell, is no more. It was too slow for this fast age and it has been sacrificed to the spirit of progress."

Brooks Bridge (Photo: Courtesy Medford Historical Society)

A Canal Scrapbook

Boston

In 1817

The improvement of the Mill-pond (which is nearly fill'd up) next claims our attention. From the old Ferry-ways [now the end of Charles River Bridge] to the mill bridge in Middle Street, a new street has been constructed, nearly eighty feet in width, on which are a number of large Brick houses. The Mill Creek or Canal is continued through [what was the Mill pond] to the old Causeway and connects the waters of Charles River with the harbour. Great quantities of merchandize and Country produce are transported on the Middlesex Canal, of which this Creek may be considered a part, to & from the Metropolis.

The Middlesex Canal unites the waters of Charles River and the Merrimack. The Banks of the latter River, and the Banks, and Ponds which empty into it, are burthened with forests of excellent timber, which are easily conveyed to Boston, and find a ready sale. So, also the heavy produce of the farms of the interior. The Middlesex Canal opens a communication with the interior of this state, and has been productive of much good.

In the town of Chelmsford, thro' which it passes. there is an extensive quarry of light coloured *granite,* which is easily split into large blocks, and wrought with facility.

These blocks are conveyed down the Canal to the States prison in Charlestown and prepared by the convicts for the builders use. The New Court house, the new South Meeting-house, several banks and public buildings and a large block of buildings fronting Bowdoin Square, and owned by Mr. Samuel Parkman are composed of this stone.

—Shubael Bell

(*An Account of the Town of Boston written in 1817,* from: Bostonian Society Publications, Vol. 3, (2nd series), 1919)

A Floating Tow-Line

A sort of floating tow-line was arranged . . . whereby the crew could pull and work the barge across [to Boston from the Charlestown millpond], but which could apparently slip easily under the hulls of sailing craft. . . . The Boston end was at Almshouse Wharf, near the northeast corner of the North Market building at Commercial Street - at that time the water's very edge.

Locks at Horn Pond (Courtesy: Woburn Public Library)

95

This was worked in the following manner: a series of heavy anchor stones were sunk along the desired route to Boston across the open water of the Charles and a stout cable supported by a substantial float extended upward from each one of them. Each cable had on it loosely a strong iron ring, the rings of successive cables being joined by a chain segment to form one continuous chain from Charlestown to Boston. Apparently each ring had a light line attaching it to the float above enabling it to be pulled upward and retrieved at any time. Thus the main chain could be "picked up" from any cable station float if it had been lost. By pulling on the chain, the barge could be worked across the open water.

—Douglas P. Adams
A River in the Sky

When the British Blockaded Boston

During the war [of 1812], the timber used to repair the *Constitution* frigate, was brought down the [Middlesex] canal to Boston, and that used to build the *Independence*, seventy-four, except the live oak, was procured through the same channel, as also were many of the masts and spars, &c. which were furnished at Boston, to our vessels of war. Without this canal, this part of the country could not have supplied these necessary articles.

—New York Canal Commission Report, 1821

Boat on the canal (Joseph Paryo)

Charlestown

A Fishing Agreement
Boston, May 1, 1812

Memorandum of agreement between J. L. Sullivan, Canal Agent, and Jonathan Page of Charlestown, Witnesseth That said Sullivan in consideration of the premises gives (conditionally) to said Page the exclusive privilege of taking fish at the Locks in Charlestown & the parts of the Canal adjacent thereto, provided and it is agreed by said Page that the said fishing shall occasion no interruption to the business of passing of the Canal - that the Gates and paddle gates shall not be opened shut or altered, that no damage whatsoever shall be done to the Locks — that the offals or dressing of the fish shall not be thrown in the Canal, nor allowed to remain near the same, nor any dead fish - that their [sic] shall be no interference with the business of the Lock Tender, who may take

Type of scows used on the old Middlesex Canal. From Boston to Lowell. Years. 1804 to 1852.

fish for his own family use—that said Page will cause an account to be taken by the Locktender of the quantity taken from time to time. And he engages to pay two shillings a barrel for those that shall be barreld, and one half of the amount of sales of fish not barreld, payment to be made as soon as the fish shall be sold, if sold the present summer, otherwise at the end of the boating season say 1st Dec next.

—Jon. Page
—J.L. Sullivan

(Middlesex Canal document, Mogan Library, Lowell)

The Canal Inspires Poets

In the summer of 1829 Samuel Jones Tuck and his wife Judith took a three months' trip through New England. She wrote a rhyming diary of the trip which began with a ride through the Middlesex Canal. This excerpt describes the start.

> Sunday the twenty-fifth of June
> It was in the morning very soon
> Over to Charlestown I did ride
> Likewise my husband by my side,
> At 8 o'clock went to the boat
> And very soon were set afloat.
> We entered on the fine canal
> Where there was neither sea nor swell,
> Now as I sat there at my ease
> Thought to myself it would you please
> If I my pen and ink should use
> And send you something to peruse.
> The scene it is so very fine
> That I can scarcely write a line,

> Oh never since I've been a wife
> Or I will say in all my life
> More beauteous sight did ever see.
> I wish you were all here with me.
> Oh how delightful is the scene
> The roses red, the grass so green,
> Variety here is so great
> It claims us much as here we sit..
> I ne'er before a Lock did see
> And of them could have no idea.
> It is a great curiosity indeed
> To see the water in full speed,
> To see how gradual and how still
> The boat doth rise up on the hill,
> Over us now dressed are the willow trees
> And many more the eye to please,
> We sailed through many a beauteous farm
> And God kept us all from harm.
> How can we view these beauties dear
> And not acknowledge, "God is near."

—Medford Historical Register
September 1933

Somerville

The Canal and the Convent

The St. Ursula Convent in Somerville was a school for girls, who came from the eastern and southern states, as well as Canada—Protestants as well as Catholics. The convent stood on Mount Benedict, which was the "Ploughed Hill" of Revolutionary history.

Only known photograph of canal boat on the canal taken when the canal was still operating.
From a glass slide in the Medford Historical Society collection.

Incited by prejudicial stories that women were held in the convent against their will, afterwards found to be untrue, a mob attacked and burned the buildings on the night of August 11,1834. The twelve nuns succeeded in getting out safely the 57 girls, most of whom were Protestants. About a dozen prominent citizens were arrested and tried for alleged participation in the affair. Only one was convicted and he later was pardoned. That October, the Ursulines bought the General Dearborn estate in Roxbury for a new convent. Portions of the ruins stood as late as 1887. The houses pictured here were on the Medford turnpike and the bridge over the canal can be seen at the foot of the hill. Later, the hill was mostly taken down and the earth was used to fill in the canal and the marshland along the Mystic River.

Ursuline Convent with canal passing at its base.

Medford

Brooks's Pleasure Ground

Although the [Middlesex] canal can be likened to a highway cutting Peter [Chardon Brooks's] property in half, it was much less intrusive than the image implies. The canal was narrow, ... at or below grade and - most importantly - completely silent. It was this latter quality that left the pastoral landscape virtually untouched and, in the minds of many, enhanced.

Peter treated the canal like a landscape element, planting hedges along its western bank and later constructing a graceful, single-arched bridge over it. The Canal Company had initially built a wooden bridge where a road leading from Peter's house to his farm had been cut in half, but in 1821 Peter replaced it with an arch of Chelmsford granite, paying the cost of $1,000 himself. The new bridge, which spanned what is now Sagamore Avenue where Sagamore Park intersects it, was widely regarded as an architectural gem due to its simplicity and elegance. It was one of the earlier designs of George Rumford Baldwin. . .

The Canal Company was understandably pleased that Peter had built and paid for a new, low-maintenance bridge at the site. With this in his favor, Peter asked for and received permission from the Canal Company to transform the shore of the Mystic Lakes from his property to beyond the Parting [of the lakes] into a "pleasure ground." By adding paths and grooming the surrounding woodlands, Peter turned the area between the lake and the canal into one of striking beauty.

Peter's pleasure ground became a popular promenade for young men and women. . .

—Michael J. Rawson
Imprints of the Past, 1997

The Canal in Winter and Summer

The Middlesex Canal in winter was very unlike the river. There was no danger in its currentless four foot water; no unfrozen margin. It always froze smooth and early, so that we were sure of skating on Thanksgiving day. . . .

West of Main street the winter canal was nicer. It generally was in sight of the river and, for a long stretch, of the Walnut tree hill on which no Tufts College or anything else stood, though I seem to remember the lone walnut tree. Beyond the aqueduct and through the woodlands it was ideal. The heavy oaks kept off the wind. We could look down upon the lovely lake which at times was very near the canal and perhaps twenty feet lower. We could climb down the slope and explore on our skates all its nooks and bays. Some distance above the "parting" there was an apron of plank, the wasteway for the surplus water of the canal. This made a handsome cascade as the water tumbled over the rocks right into the upper pond. . . .

In the summer the canal was delightful also. No place could be more beautiful that the mile or two of its passage through the lake woodlands. The great boats never charged us passage money and at every bridge one could step on or off a boat. . . . With the eyes shut you could not say there was any motion. The boatmen never bothered us. They had little to do but talk. Theirs was in general easy service. The long tow had the horse at one end, and the other was made fast to the top of a slightly elastic pole which stood near but not quite at the middle of the boat's length. Its exact position was scientifically important, for if it was rightly placed the boat would keep the middle of the water, and only at approaching a bridge or another boat did the boatman need to lean against his enormous steering oar.

The fishing in the canal must be noticed. Pickerel were there, and the troller had an easy time loafing along the tow path from which he could cover all the water. Smaller fish were numerous at certain spots, notably at the Lowell railroad bridge which crossed the canal near the arch over the river. Here were beam, perch, shiners, etc., but no pouts. The pouts were about ten feet south of the canal in a little pond at the angle of the railroad and canal. and there they were plenty. . . .

The pleasantest and most productive of the fishing places was at and near Mr. Brook's granite arch. . . . The arch was perfect in its absolute simplicity. A gravel path from the Brooks mansion led over it and onward along the west bank of the canal to the nearest part of the lake where was Mr. Brooks' grove extending from the canal to the lake, full of similar trees of great size, and with pretty paths and two little stone arches over a bit of the brook which flowed down to the lake. We did not fish in the canal beyond this, but the cool shadow of the granite arch, where no sun ray ever came, was with the adjoining tree shadows, a favorite home of many kinds of fish. Besides the striped perch and bream,

Going into the lock (Joseph Payro)

we there took cheven, a rather larger fish, all silver and resembling a scup, suckers large enough if not very good, and chub. This last had large silver scales with a sort of purple iridescence, and would sometimes weigh a pound. They were very good eating too. Another beautiful fish was found at this bridge and only here. It was about as large as a small smelt, silvery but with crimson tipped fins and tail.

—Thomas M. Stetson (born 1830)
An Old School Boy's Reminiscences
Medford Historical Register, Oct. 1914

Winchester

Something Gone

In [the canal] we boys learned to swim in summer, and on its surface we took our first lessons in skating. We caught fish in its waters, navigated rafts, had rides with friendly boatmen, and spent most of our leisure hours along its banks. From the time the water was drawn off in the fall, leaving only shallow pools to mark its course, to the filling in the spring, we longed for its reappearing, and when one spring came and lengthened into summer, and the water did not rise we felt as though something had gone out of our lives.

—"An old-timer"
Winchester Star, 1900

Mosquitoes Too

This long ditch was dug for boys to swim in, as well as boats, and from all along its friendly banks, and beneath the shade and gracefulness of hanging foliage, fresh and green and lovely, bathers in joyous splash and noisy daring would cool their sweaty limbs and vie with each other in aquatic sport.

Sometimes a special thirst would incline us to drink from the flowing flood. But, before partaking, a quick glance would assure us that no inanimate dog or cat or hen, was slowly floating upon the contaminated bosom of this commercial ribbon. And when a boat hove in sight, and a driver was on the tow-path, to prod the horses' energies, we were quick to leave the water, seize our apparel, and make for the adjacent thickets.

Then further, it would seem, the mosquitoes quenched their thirst from this convenient water. For, if at evening, young men went to bathe in the canal, it was always remarkable with what freedom the mosquitoes would feed upon the anatomy of the bathers. With a kind of stifled hum, the enemy would fix upon his prey, and bore for the vital fluid, and the victim would strike for his enemy. And so, this canal ... was suited to sail boats in, uphill and down, for a natatorium for country boys, and a stream from which mosquitoes could drink when they couldn't bite the blithe and happy bathers.

—Old Native
Winchester Star
April 15, 1910

Woburn

Frolicking Boys

Boys used to have fine fun in swimming close up to the lower gates [of a lock], when a boat was coming down, and 'treading water' or 'floating on their backs' waiting for the flood gates to be opened; when this was done, the powerful streams rushing out would tumble them over and over like frogs, amid the screeching and laughter of the little swimmers, as they 'brought up' some distance below.

—Parker L. Converse
Legends of Woburn, 2nd series

The Old Tow Path

The old tow-path was a sort of enchanting walk, of which, when the Canal was open for navigation, a large number of people availed themselves. In Winter, too, when it was frozen up, it was a skating 'rink' many times better than any other in town. I will only add that, with all my appreciation of the superior value of railroads, I have never become fully reconciled to the abandonment of the old Middlesex Canal.

—Parker L. Converse
Legends of Woburn, 2nd series

Loammi Baldwin

When water was first admitted into the canal as far as Woburn meeting house, the following lines slightly adapted from Dr. Erasmus Darwin, appeared in the Columbian Centinel *for July 10, 1802:*

So with strong arm immortal Baldwin leads
His long canals and parts the velvet meads;
Winding in lucid lines the watery mass,
Mines the firm rock, or loads the deep morass,
With rising locks a thousand hills alarms,
Flings o'er a thousand streams its silver arms,
Feeds the long vale, the nodding woodland laves,
And plenty, arts and commerce fright the waves.

Lively Horn Pond

From a letter by G. Cheney, a Woburn school teacher, to his friend Brother Moody, written in Woburn, Aug. 11, 1840:

Since I came out of school this afternoon I have been down to Horn Pond and about. It is a most delightful place, but like all other good things of Creation of Providence, much abused by man. A pond of 12 or 15 acres (for a rough guess) surrounded on all sides, except a part of it toward my window with verdant groves, a fine place for bathing, fishing, and sailing. Close along side of it are four locks of the Middlesex Canal, one of which built of hammered stone is the fairest stone work I ever saw. There is a tavern with a thousand accommodations, conveniences and entertainments to allure the city-killed gentry. The summer house and bathing house, the boats for sculling and the shady walk, the ropes for swinging and the alley for bowling, at which last a large business is carried on.

I saw a few weeks ago in the hottest weather, Boston ladies rolling or attempting to roll lignum vitae balls 5 or 6 inches in diameter, the thermometer probably at 95! Thousands of people visit here every year by individuals, families, military companies, religious societies, and Indian tribes. A tribe of Penobscots was here a few days ago. They bro't their birch bark canoes and stayed several days, the squaws making baskets and selling them.

Towpath Topics, v. 17, n. 1

Wilmington

A Sinking Embankment

At a place called the sinking meadow, in [Wilmington], an embankment is made across a marsh of about 30 rods in extent.

When this embankment was commenced, it was found that the dirt and stuff carried on, to form the embankment kept gradually sinking into the marsh; when measures were taken to ascertain how much it would sink: the labourers continued to carry on stuff which gradually went down, until the whole embankment sunk to the depth of 60 feet!

The great expense of making this embankment across the marsh, might have been foreseen, and prevented. The depth and softness of the marsh, might have been ascertained by sounding it with an iron rod, and by conducting the canal circuitously around its margin, a solid foundation might have been secured.

Documents relating to the New-York Canals, 1821

Rustle Up The Grub!

Micajah Cowing (1790–1864) tended Gillis Lock in Wilmington for some years. His son, Daniel Cowing, (1821–1902) took over and was tending the lock in 1847 when his mother died. He shortly married Sarah Ames in 1848. She went there as a bride in March 1848, nineteen years old, and ran the Inn for boatmen and boarders besides. Her sisters and Daniel's sisters helped her.

The story was often told at Gowing family reunions of how the boatmen would blow the whistle when they came into Wilmington from Woburn indicating how many passengers would need lunch at the Inn when the canal boat arrived at Gillis Lock.

—Christine C. Allard
Letter to the authors
June 9, 1997

Billerica

Floating Bridge Pier

In 1912, the Concord River at the Talbot mill-pond was being drawn down to its lowest stage. Harry G. Sheldon took a number of photographs of the nearly empty pond, including this one which shows one of the two piers which supported the eastern end of the Floating Bridge.

This is a close-up of the outer pier, with one side of the inner pier showing. Note the hand-hewn timbers used for the construction of the main pier. It was weighted down with stone. The mortised corners are still intact and solid. Note the silt that has collected around the wooden timbers of the pier. These piers were sunk several feet into the soil. Note the almost perfect condition

of the timbers after having been in place for more than 110 years.

—C. Talbot Sheldon
Notes on the Photographs
Mogan Library, Lowell

Chelmsford

The Only Living Person

I have been told that, some time in my first year, my mother made the voyage [on the canal], taking me with her when she went to visit Madame Dalton at her house, No. 82 Mt. Vernon St., Boston. If this is true—and I have no reason to doubt it—I probably enjoy the distinction of being the only living person who arrived in Boston by a canal-boat. But I do not claim any great merit on this account.

—Rev. Wilson Waters
The History of Chelmsford, 1917

A Sunday on the Canal, Sept. 1, 1839

We here left its channel [the Concord River], just above the Billerica Falls and entered the canal, which runs, or rather is conducted, six miles through the woods to the Merrimack at Middlesex, and as we did not care to loiter in this part of our voyage, while one ran along the towpath drawing the boat by a cord, the other kept off the shore with a pole, so that we accomplished the whole distance in little more than an hour. This canal, which is the oldest in the country, and has even an antique look beside the more modern railroads, is fed by the Concord, so that we were still floating on its familiar waters. It is so much water which the river *lets* for the advantage of commerce.

There appeared some want of harmony in its scenery, since it is not of equal date with woods and meadows through which it is led, and we missed the conciliatory influence of time on land and water; but in the lapse of ages, Nature will recover and indemnify herself, and gradually plant fit shrubs and flowers along its borders. Already the Kingfisher sat upon a pine over the water, and the bream and pickerel swam below. Thus all works pass directly out of the hand of the architect into the hands of Nature, to be perfected. . . .

As we passed under the last bridge over the canal, just before reaching the Merrimack, the people coming out of the church paused to look at us from above, and apparently, so strong is custom [against Sunday travel], indulged in some heathenish comparisons. . .

—Henry David Thoreau
A Week on the Concord and Merrimack Rivers, 1849

Picnic by the canal. Wall mural by Zena Bernstein, private collection.

Middlesex Village (Lowell)

The Locks at Middlesex Village

That part of the Canal, which is in Chelmsford is 25 feet above the waters of the Merrimack River, from which you ascend by means of three locks formed of split stone, laid in mortar. "The lock next to the river is called the first lock. This is ninety feet long and twelve wide. The earth is removed below the bed of the river to prevent the undermining of the works, and then filled up with stones, on these a floor of oak timber, two feet square is laid; upon this another floor of similar timber is laid cross wise, and then a floor of three inch planks, all well spiked and trunnelled.

Grooves cut in rock by canal boat ropes as they went around the Oxbow bend in the Wilmington Town Forest.

On this base the walls are raised 8 feet high and 7 feet thick. The walls are constructed of hewn stone, taken from a ledge in the neighborhood, which is the property of the corporation. These stones are easily split, and readily yield to the stroke of the hammer. The second and third locks are of the same length, and constructed of similar materials. The height of the second is 16, that of the third 14 feet. The culverts and gates are so well contrived, that a boat or raft may pass the three locks in 8 minutes. The workmanship of these locks for neatness and strength is equalled by none in the United States.

The naturalist will be gratified to learn that on digging over the earth on the bank of Merrimack river, to lay the foundation of the locks, pine cones and charcoal were found at the depth of twelve feet from the surface, in a sound and unimpaired state, specimens of which are deposited in the museum at Cambridge. A small horn was also found at nearly the same depth from the surface, supposed to be that of a cow of two or three years old.

—William Allen
The History of Chelmsford, 1820

Water Usage

The canal descended one inch per mile, causing a current of about half a mile an hour. Every time a lock was discharged at the outlet at Charlestown, Medford, or Middlesex Village, 50,000 gallons of water was lost; and, at the latter place, three times as much when a boat passed up through the locks. A record kept there showed the locks operated 6,000 times a year. The quantity of water lost by evaporation and filtration was estimated at 50 cubic feet per minute. The amount necessary for the locks and evaporation was estimated at 10,960,000 gallons per day, or nearly 15.4 cubic feet per second for 24 hours. In addition to this, a large amount of water flowed over waste weirs, and the lock tenders had to draw on the level above to maintain a proper level in the section under their control. The amount estimated for this purpose was 2,000,000 gallons per day per mile, or 3.1 cubic feet per second for 28 miles equal to 86.8 cubic feet per second for 24 hours. This amount added to the locks and evaporation equals 102.2 cubic feet per second for 24 hours. In August 1830, it was found that the current through the Shawsheen aqueduct had a velocity of 3 minutes 30 seconds in a distance of 180 feet 3 inches.

—Lewis M. Lawrence
The Middlesex Canal, 1942

Memories

Mention should be made of its "locks," the number of which I cannot recall, but the solidity of some, notably those in Woburn, north of Horn Pond, I shall never forget, now with what interest and excitement I used to see them filled and "drawn off" to serve the passing of the boats from a higher to a lower level or vice versa.

In this canal was I wont to cast the dainty lure and practice my first lesson in the "gentle art" of angling.On its shady banks how often have I watched the laden barges approach and slowly fade away in the pretty and umbrageous vista and listened to the splash of the mimic waves their sluggish passing caused. . . .

I never see a bit of its crumbling, over-grown, or filled-up "bed," but I think of the pleasure once afforded by a quiet, dreamy day "on the canal."It would not suit a "nervous" temperament, nor one in hot haste, but to one *not* in haste, who loved nature and had a "quiet conscience," what a restful, enjoyable experience it must have been. With congenial company, a pleasant book for odd moments, with ample time for every duty, or inclination, with the mild excitement of "locking" (passage through the

locks), the day need not have been too long, nor the "voyage" wearisome.

It is vain to wish for it - it can never be!

—Oliver W, Rogers
The Middlesex Hearthstone, May 1896

Moosehead Lake, Maine

The Lost Canal Townships

Some 260 miles north of Boston, nestled along the rocky, rugged shoreline of Moosehead Lake, Maine, lie two vast tracts of timeberland and ponds. Uninhabited, undeveloped, and mostly undisturbed, they are much the same as in 1809 when they became forever linked to the story of the Middlesex Canal. In that year, abandoning a standing policy that forbade financial assistance to private enterprise, the General Court of Massachusetts granted two townships in the District of Maine to the Proprietors of the Middlesex Canal.

At that time the precarious fiscal state of the Canal Corporation, worsened by the Embargo of 1808, would not allow them to proceed with construction of a canal system on the Merrimack River. Such a system was considered critical to the success of their entire inland waterway scheme. Thus the General Court was induced to grant these northern lands of the Canal Corporation, funds from the anticipated sales of the Moosehead plots, each nearly 36 square miles in size, were to be used to help finance the Merrimack River canals. The anticipated value of the plots was some $17,000.

The East and West Middlesex Canal Townships, while supplying a much-needed boost to sagging morale, were far too remote to be of any real value to the company financially. The Directors wisely sought other methods to finance their canal system, although they gratefully accepted the two well-intended parcels. It comes as no surprise that the hiring of a survey team to lay out the proper bounds of the townships did not occur until early in 1816.

Try as they might, the Middlesex Canal Company was many years in disposing of their Moosehead townships. Finally, in 1831, the wilderness holdings were sold to a Samuel Bradley for a mere $9,000. The bulk of this sum was paid in notes of credit to the corporation. They were likely never paid in full.

Recently, I was able to strike out in search of the lost townships, both now part of the vast Maine real estate holdings of the Great Northern Paper Company. Soaring above the two ancient grants in a small pontoon airplane was an awesome experience. The canal townships sit at opposite bands of Moosehead's North Bay. The seemingly endless vista of mountains, ponds, streams, and bogs remains as rugged as it must have been in 1816, when that first survey team had to conquer them. . .

An aerial overview, however, was not the way in which I wanted to search for tangible reminders of the brief association of this vast wilderness with our remarkable ditch. Like any dedicated "canawler," I took to the ground. Following a narrow, muddy logging road, virtually the only modern intrusion, through the West Middlesex Canal Township, I made good use of a topographical map and some dead-reckoning. I made my way past Tomhegan Pond and crossed Socatean Stream in the hopes of locating one of the boundary posts of our "lost" townships. The undergrowth, or "pucker-brush" was tough and the insects tougher. This was something that only a Middlesex Canal "nut" would undertake.

Then, quite unexpectedly, I came across that for which I had been hoping. There, rising out of the deep, close forest, was the tangible link I had sought between the canal and the woods - the

boundary marker. It was a moment for reflection. The Canal Corporation had come and gone. Yet the old canal itself endures, and so, too, do the 'lost" Middlesex Canal Townships.

—Tom Smith
Towpath Topics, v. 26, n. 2

Farewell

As the canal was being "drawn off"—that is, closing down in 1853— the following poem by someone who styled themselves "Timoon" appeared in the Woburn Journal *for Oct. 23, 1853. It makes a fitting sentimental close to our Canal Scrapbook.*

Our Old Canal

Thou old canal! thou old canal!
    We seek thee now in vain;
No more thou glidest through the hills,
    Or wet'st the verdant plain.
No more upon thy banks shall grow,
    With foliage fresh and green;
The clust'ring alder or the birch,
    Or the whispering pine between.
The flowerets, too, no more shall spring,
    Or raise their fragrant heads,
To watch their faces in thy breast,
    From off their smiling beds.
Full many a year thy waters flowed,
    But now - they'll flow no more;
Thy bed is dry, and parched too,
    And broken is thy shore.
Thy shelving basins, once so fair,

Are now to gardens turned;
And thy quaint locks are nigh torn down,
    And given to be burned.
Upon thy banks fond lovers now,
    At eve no more shall go;
To spend the dewy hours there,
    In converse soft and low.
But desolation sere and dread,
    There stalketh forth at eve;
And revels where rough bushes grow,
    To which rude brambles cleave.
The Scots may sing of Avon dear,
    And sweetly hymn its praise;
But thee I knew and prized in youth,
    Thou playmate of those days!
Thou wert an Avon then to me,
    And though thou'rt passed away,
Thou'lt be *my* Avon still for aye,
    Throughout life's mazy day.
Thou old canal! thou old canal!
    Oh! who my grief can tell,
As from my heart I bid thee now,
    A long—a sad farewell.

Boys flying a kite by the canal. Wall mural by Zena Bernstein, private collection.

View of the old Middlesex Canal, before 1912. Courtesy of the Society for the Preservation of New England Antiquites. The authors believe this photograph was taken by Colonel Loammi Baldwin's great-grandson, Baldwin Coolidge. (1845-1928)

Locks at Horn Pond, Woburn, as visualized by Thomas Dahill.

4/10/86 Middlesex Village

Middlesex Village as visualized by Thomas Dahill.

Samuel Abbott's Landing in Woburn Center as imagined by Louis Linscott.

Afterglow–Since Closure

Even before the canal was discontinued, there were some who wanted to save it. On Oct. 17, 1850, Edward Everett—he who had been governor and senator from Massachusetts and now was President of Harvard—went into Boston to talk with Edward Brooks. His father having died, Edward now owned the land in Medford through which the canal passed. As Everett wrote in his diary, "I suggested to him the expediency of buying the franchise rather than to allow a river of twenty five miles in length to be filled up. He said the purchase would be attended with heavy liabilities connected with keeping the locks and water ways in repair." That sober financial fact was enough to discourage the President of Harvard— and others who thought as he did.

So it was that on Nov. 25, 1851 the last boat traveled the full length of the Middlesex Canal. It was in charge of Samuel King. After that all maintenance on the canal ceased. There were no lockkeepers. Taverns closed for lack of business from boatmen and holiday makers. Fishermen still cast their lines into the canal, and where it froze in winter, people continued to skate on it. In winter, nearby farmers cut ice from the canal. But the daily passage of boats ceased, and quiet settled over its route.

Almost immediately people felt a sense of nostalgia for the "old canal." The Woburn Journal for August 18, 1855 began the process.

It is all over now with the old Middlesex Canal. The demoniac shriek of the Lowell express-train, reverberates above its empty bed. Our style of getting about is vastly altered, and we tear and roar through the country at forty miles an hour. When we look back to catch a glimpse of the country through which we rush, we are rewarded with a cinder in our eye, and are forced to drop a tear of regret. . . . Modern America is in altogether too much of a hurry for happiness, and can scarcely conceive of the quiet enjoyment of a day on the Middlesex Canal. 3 miles an hour, stops included.

With the abandonment of the canal, all upkeep ceased. People watched it decay. For when the canal went out of business, when it in effect "died," it was not taken away and buried. It did not disappear instantly. It sat there in its bed and gradually disintegrated, bit by bit, piece by piece, section by section.

No one cleared the grass out of the waterway. Shrubs and small trees began to grow up along the canal banks and on the towpath. Trees fell across the canal. With no one keeping the muskrats in check, they bored nesting holes into the banks. Decay settled in along the length of the old canal. Moses W, Mann, moving to

Medford in early 1870, described the sad condition of Gilson's lock in West Medford:

> An enormous willow, over four feet in diameter, and several sycamores shaded the spot, while the great stone walls of the canal lock, overrun with blackberry vines and filled with a growth of bushes, told the story of the passing of the old waterway. This was accentuated by the slowly decaying timbers of the aqueduct across the river, from whose supporting braces hung the sedge grass left by the flood tide. Empty for nearly twenty years, it had been exposed to the decaying forces of nature and it was a picturesque ruin.

Bathing beach on north bank of canal in North Billerica, near High Street

Such a description would have been typical of all the surviving locks and aqueducts along the canal route.

Yet in some areas, there was a lot of activity on the canal. In places where land was most in demand, particularly at either end of the canal near Boston and Lowell, people began filling in its empty bed. The mill pond at Charlestown, the canal's southern terminal, was quickly filled up. As had happened to the Back Bay in Boston, the Charlestown mill pond became a kind of dump, and after 1872 was filled by the Eastern Railroad, so that Charlestown now reached over to Cambridge. Rutherford Avenue was constructed through the area about the same time. Railroads tracks were laid down where the mill pond had been graded over and filled.

Moving out from Charlestown, the same filling process happened to most of the canal where it ran through Somerville. Likewise in Medford. Boston Avenue filled in the old canal bed and Gilson's Lock by 1875. In 1896 Combination Park, a race track, had been built over much of the old canal bed in South Medford. Winchester, which in 1850 had been incorporated from parts of Medford, Arlington, and Woburn, also began to convert the abandoned canal bed to additional land. Wildwood Cemetery included part of the canal when it was laid out in the 1852. Along Horn Pond and up to Woburn Center the same filling-in process continued.

At the other end of the canal, Middlesex Village, which had been part of Chelmsford, had now become part of Lowell, and the basin on the Merrimack where boats gathered to begin their journey down the canal to Boston was filled in by the railroad.

There it seemed to stop. In Woburn, North Woburn, Wilmington, Billerica, and Chelmsford - towns further out from Boston - there was not in the last half of the nineteenth century, the immediate demand for land. They had to wait for their development in the twentieth century.

But people didn't forget the old canal. For some it sat in their backyards, and they took occasional strolls along it. Young people who grew up after the canal had ceased operations became fascinated by its history. They talked to their older neighbors and heard stories of the good old canal days.

At the end of the canal's life, photography became available. The Medford Historical Society has a photograph of a canal boat being towed along the canal by a horse while the canal was still operating.. This is the only known photograph from that period, and must have been taken by a professional with his bulky equipment. Half of an old stereoptican slide of the Red Lock in Chelmsford has survived. This was after the canal was abandoned, but still very early.

Once cameras became smaller and easier to use, people began to take pictures of various sites along the canal. The same Moses Mann who had recorded in words the decay of Gilson's lock, much later, got out his camera and recorded much of what remained of the canal from its great days. His glass slides were given to the Middlesex Canal Association (MCA) by Mrs. Wendell Dykeman, a grand-daughter or niece who was then living in Annisquam. She had heard about the MCA from the newspapers and contacted them. Mrs. Dykeman had gone around with Mann when he lectured about the canal and at intermissions in the program played her banjo. The glass slides were in a box which Mann had made from a piece of wooden timber he found in the Mystic River that had been part of the aqueduct over the canal at what is now the Boston Avenue bridge.

Mann's photos were taken about the turn of the century, some forty years after the canal's abandonment. Other people also took pictures of various spots along the canal. Pictures of the toll house in Middlesex Village, and of the Shawsheen aqueduct, were taken in the 1890s by unknown photographers. Harry G. Sheldon took photos of the canal from 1893 to 1912 and these came to the MCA in 1968.

Professional photographer Baldwin Coolidge, a descendant of Loammi Baldwin, also made some photographs of the canal in the years between 1889 and 1906. By then, it seemed as if everybody was out recording what was left of the canal in snapshots. The Mogan Center in Lowell has 35 photos taken by James L. Faden in the early 1930s. Charles F. Morey's scrapbooks from the same period have photos of the canal.

Another photographic survey of the canal in the 1930s, can be found in the Tufts Archives. Here are five loose-leaf notebooks prepared by Melville Munro, then Professor of Electrical Engineering at the college. He died in 1945. The notebooks are in two sets (two one-volume and one three-volume). The first consists of a brief typescript of the Canal illustrated by over 90 photographs. The second, a typed running commentary of 123 pages interspersed with pictures, also includes a 17 page "Touring Description of the Route of the Old Middlesex Canal from Lowell to Boston." The notebooks were assembled between 1932 and 1937.

There were also people sketching and drawing the canal. There is a wonderfully atmospheric painting by an E. T. Baker, who was active from 1850 to 1875, of a canal boat being locked through during sunset. It is thought to be the Middlesex Canal that was depicted. This painting is now in a private collection.

The New England Magazine for January, 1898, had a long account of the canal, and for this they had an artist by the name of Marshall Tidd make a number of pencil sketches of boats and rafts and places along the canal. These were later reproduced by the Middlesex Canal Association as notepaper.

Louis R. Linscott (1876-1966) of Woburn, was an artist, designer, and illustrator. He spent four years studying art in Paris and London. In 1902 he married Catherine Wilkie Bennet of

London, England. They had two daughters, Dorothy and Virginia, who followed him in his profession. For many years he drew historical sketches of old Woburn which were published in the annual calendars of the S. B. Goddard & Son Co. Through these scenes he made the Middlesex Canal, a stretch of which ran near his home in North Woburn, familiar to thousands of people. The Linscott Art Collection is now at the Mogan Center in Lowell. Eleven of his sketches were published by the Middlesex Canal Association in 1978.

Joseph C. Payro (1862-1953) a history buff who lived in Wakefield, was born in Montreal. As a young child he moved to Lowell with his parents, where he worked in the cotton mills. In his late teens he traveled to New York and worked for a short time on the Erie Canal driving the mules that drew a canal boat. His experience resulted in a life-long interest in canals. After his return to Massachusetts he settled in Wakefield, and for many

Canal in Woburn with railroad tracks running alongside it.

years was connected with the Heywood Wakefield Furniture Company as an artist and craftsman. With his friends, Morison Merrill (town engineer of Wakefield) and Leon Cutler (who gave lectures on the canal in the 1930s and died in the 1940s), he explored the route of the canal and took many photographs of it. He also copied old maps and drawings of the canal. He made three paintings of the canal now at the Mogan Center.

There were now quite a few people walking along the canal. The first recorded walk was on March 26, 1921, led by Edith Coverly. This was followed by two walks in November 1922, and one in December 1923, led by Mr. Van Everen. He also led three walks on May 30, and November 1 and 15, 1924. In July 1924, Mr. Chamberlain led an Appalachian Mountain Club group in the area of the canal. These continued for many years, and now are taken in conjunction with the Middlesex Canal Association.

An anonymous ramble along the canal was taken in December 1923 and latter written up . The manuscript does not indicate the author but perhaps it was Mr. Van Everen who walked the canal that month. It describes the state of the canal in that year. At that time the old toll house was still standing in Middlesex Village. "Through the Mt. Pleasant Golf Links to Chelmsford Street the canal is very much in evidence with water enough to support fish life" The account includes such quaint remarks as "The trolley line from Gorham Street to North Billerica is probably along the tow path as the bed of the canal at the left is clearly discernible." And in North Woburn it describes the canal entering " the Italian Village with its picturesque grape trellises."

Mal Wood wrote up in June 1931 an account of several walks he took along the old Middlesex Canal with various companions. His account was found in the collection of Edward Carney at the Lowell Historical Society. He had a vivid eye and ear for the natural life to be found along the abandoned canal in the last years of the 1920s. Here is a spring memory of what he saw and heard in the River Meadows section of the canal in Chelmsford:

> In the spring of the year the meadows roundabout are flooded, only the towpath, the eshers, and the causeway standing out high and dry above the swales. Cat-o-nine-tails invite bob-o-links, redwings, and all the less flashy tribe of migrants and visitors to this birds' paradise. Tanagers and finches frequent the oaks along the dry ridges. Fishermen from time to time venture phlegmatically out into the marsh, following the curving stream in search of finny prey. Kingfishers and hawks eye them insolently, glorying in flight. The turquoise sky is winrowed with fleecy clouds, as though Asgard were bleaching a fair white crop of pearly hay in the fields of heaven. A mackerel sky at sunset is often reflected in purple and magenta, rose and gold in the pools of the marsh. It is a spot to be frequently visited, a feast of beauty to revel in, full of ecstatic moments and long hours of sunlight falling with fruitful benison over the wide earth.

Such a picture gives us an idea of what those travelling up and down the old canal would have seen and heard in its days of busy activity.

When Wood came to the Shawsheen aqueduct, he found a more rural picture than we meet with today.

> The canal bed is here about ten feet above the Wilmington-Billerica road [route 129], which is close at hand. It is a warm spot—the canal traverses mostly hot sandy country despite frequent swampy stretches—but the river is fairly inviting. It is reddish colored from vegetable matter and by iron ore in its sluggish swales, but cool in spring and fall. Further up, it is dammed for a private swimming pool, but here I made use of a secluded, if not a private, reach that is deep enough for swimming, and found welcome relief from the first hot day of summer.

The younger boys [accompanying Wood] enjoyed the spot immensely. They set sticks afloat as warships, and bombarded them from the safe heights above. A truck speeding past, along a seldom traveled road, gave them a thrill as it rumbled over the narrow, dangerous bridge, and displayed a red-lettered panel, "Danger, Explosives." Evidently the driver was not worried, if the speed at which he struck the rickety wooden planking were any indication.

In 1938, Professor Dirk J. Struik of the Massachusetts Institute of Technology and Clinton H. Collester led three walks along the canal all the way to Lowell.

It was time for somebody to write a scholarly history of the canal. Caleb Eddy had written a short historical sketch of the canal in 1843, but nothing had been done since, except the various accounts of walks taken along the canal and short casual accounts of the canal.

In 1938 the finest account of the canal appeared. This was written by Christopher Roberts. Roberts was born in Newark, New Jersey in 1897. During the first world war he served in France in the American Friends Relief Unit, and was a Captain in the American Red Cross. He did his undergraduate work at Haverford College where he got his B.S. in 1920. He became a doctoral candidate at Harvard in economics in the mid- nineteen twenties and received his doctorate in 1927. His doctoral dissertation was on "The Middlesex Canal." This subject had been suggested to him by Professor Edwin F. Gay and was based on the fact that the research of Walter R. Harper had uncovered the official records of the Middlesex Canal Corporation. Basing his work on this hitherto unused manuscript sources and a collection of Baldwin family manuscripts, now in Baker Library, which Roberts discovered, he put together a solid history of this initial experiment in corporate organization and of the relations of a public utility to the state and community it served.

In 1929 Roberts began teaching economics at Duke University and continued there through 1935. In 1930 he had traveled through England and France doing further canal research work. By 1936 he was back in Mather House working on transforming his dissertation into a book. During this time he was a lecturer on economics at Harvard. The book was published in 1938 by Harvard University Press as volume 61 in its economic studies series. It sold for what looks like the relatively modest price of $3.00, but this was in the years of the Great Depression when workers lived on $10 a week and were elated to earn $15, so it was the equivalent of a $50 book today. The book is dedicated to "W.R.," his father, Weldon Roberts.

Instead of returning to teaching, he joined his father's firm in Newark, the Weldon Roberts Rubber Company. During the second world war he worked in the lend-lease division of the Department of Commerce in Washington, D.C. and in their Bureau of Statistics. In 1946-7, he was in Berlin, Germany as an economic advisor for the U. S. government. He then became a vice-president of the Weldon Roberts Company living overseas in Europe. In 1949 he died of a heart attack in Vervey, Switzerland. His only survivor was a brother, Garrett. But this 242 page volume - his only known work - remains as a monument to him, and a vital resource to students of the Middlesex Canal.

An equally useful account was written shortly afterwards by Lewis M. Lawrence (1878-1945). He graduated from MIT in 1900

as an architect. He married Helen Pauline Rembert in 1903. Most of his life he worked as an architect in Boston. He lived in Melrose from 1914 until his death. In the 1930s he worked for the Historical American Buildings Survey. During this period he did a number of drawings of canal elements (aqueducts, tollbooth, and boat). This interest in the canal led him to write a competent 148 page study of the canal which he self-published in mimeographed form in 1942. Copies were deposited in many area libraries. The Canal Association republished this in 1997.

A third and more popular account of the canal was written by Mary Stetson Clarke (1911-1994), also of Melrose. This is the one most widely available today. She had written many children's stories, at least one of them dealing with the canal, *The Limner's Daughter*. A resident of Melrose nearly all her life, she was fondly known as "Mrs. Melrose." She graduated from Melrose High school in 1929, and from Boston University in 1933. Graduate work at Columbia University followed, then she worked as an advertising copywriter for the Christian Science *Monitor* for four years. The mother of three children, she was active in many community organizations and was a trustee of the local library for 21 years. She began writing books at the age of 40, mostly historical novels and non-fiction. She has written more than a dozen, including *The Old Middlesex Canal,* which was first published in 1974, and is now in its second edition. In her last years she and her husband Edwin moved to Scituate to be near family members.

Over the years, many people became enthusiasts of the canal. Among these were Charles Frederic Morey of Billerica (d. 1949) A lifelong canal buff, he knew its entire length. His grandfather had been engaged in the wood business in Tewksbury, and used to deliver fire-wood to Boston by canal boat. He prepared a scrapbook with photos of the canal and wrote an article describing the canal in the late 1930s. He and his sister, Mrs. Mary Morey Jacobs of Billerica, were descendants of Samuel Morey, the inventor of the steamboat.

Edward B. Carney was one of the acknowledged sources for Christopher Roberts' book. He collected much canal memorabilia, which is now part of the collection at the Mogan Center in Lowell.

Harry J. Lasher (1896-1973), was an artist, designer, and engineer. Born in Bennington, VT, he grew up in Hinsdale, NH. He was a graduate of Union College, Schenectady, NY, and a veteran of the First World War. His working career was spent with White's Machine Designers, Jackson and Moreland, Raytheon, and the Lowell Technological Research Foundation. He married Dorothy I. Hall in 1951 with whom he made his home in Tewksbury, MA While commuting to Boston, he noticed remnants of the old canal, appreciated its engineering significance, and began extensive research into it. One of his projects was a highly decorated map of the canal to which he devoted more than one hundred hours. It is now at the Mogan Center in Lowell.

A well-informed and enthusiastic speaker, he gave illustrated talks to historical societies and civic groups on the canal and other subjects. In 1962 he concluded a talk about the canal to the Billerica Historical Society with a rousing call to action to save what remained of the canal before it should be completely destroyed. That evening some of his listeners took the first step toward the formation of the Middlesex Canal Association.

Shawsheen Aqueduct, looking northeast, Middlesex Canal, Wilmington/ Billerica, MA. Photograph by Arthur Haskell, early 20th century. Courtesy of the Society for the Preservation of New England Antiquites.

Haulin' Down To Boston On the Middlesex Canal

Used by permission of David Dettinger

New Life-New Interest

The Middlesex Canal Association

On July 26, 1962, at an evening meeting in the old Richardson School House, now the East Billerica Community Center, a group met to adopt a set of by-laws, elect officers, and thus the Middlesex Canal Association was launched. Arthur L. Eno Jr. was elected the first president. The chartered objectives of the Association are to recognize and preserve the Middlesex Canal for public, educational, and recreational use. The Association was officially incorporated by the state on May 27, 1964.

From the very beginning one of their first priorities was to secure what remained of the canal and protect it from destruction by developers or vandalism. To that end, Mr. Eno convinced Eldred Field, then owner of the Faulkner Mills, into giving the section of North Billerica canal land that the mill owned to the Billerica Historical Society. Since the Canal Association was a new organization, Fields preferred that the ownership be in an established organization. The Association also pursued other canal land, especially railroad land, but after long negotiations, these efforts failed for a variety of reasons. Later land was given to the Association by the

Dignon family in Billerica and the Webber family in Wilmington. The Billerica Historical Society also owns the Shawsheen aqueduct.

A second goal of the Association was to publicize the canal. The custom of spring and fall walks along various sections of the canal quickly developed. In this they were joined by members of the Appalachian Mountain Club who had already been sponsoring such walks. The Boy Scout troops of the area often prepared the area for the walks. Another aspect of the publicity was to produce a newsletter, and by October 1963 the first edition of "Canal News" appeared. By the second volume this was retitled "Towpath Topics," the name it still bears.

A third goal of the Association was to collect artifacts and documents of the canal. The Billerica Historical Society gave them a room in which to collect such material and each issue of "Towpath Topics" would report on new additions to the collection. In 1970 the collection was transferred to the care of the Lydon Library at what is now the University of Massachusetts at Lowell, under the supervision of the librarian Joseph Kopycinski.

When the Massachusetts legislature annulled the 1793 charter of the Middlesex Canal Corporation in 1860, the Middlesex County Court took possession of the proprietors' records to protect them "for the use and benefit of all parties interested therein."

Song by David Dettinger, written for the 1993 Bicentennial Celebration

For 112 years they were stored at the courthouse in Cambridge. Then in 1972, the Canal Association convinced the county commissioners to add them to the collection at the Lydon Library. The transfer ceremony was held in a big tent. Shortly afterwards, Kopycinski and staff began the arduous process of unfolding, flattening, and making these neglected records available. In 1982, Thomas C. Proctor, who had selected the canal for his master's thesis, took an archival course, and in October 1983 began the process of arranging these records in archival fashion and writing a guide or finding aid to explain that arrangement. His task was completed in April 1984.

In 1989, the Patrick J. Mogan Cultural Center was opened in Lowell to tell the human story of the United States as an industrial nation, and especially to concentrate on the lives of the working people of Lowell. Housed in a former boarding house of the Boott Mill, the Center was rehabilitated by the Department of the Interior, and the Middlesex Canal collection was moved from the Lydon Library to spacious quarters in the Mogan Center where it is available for scholars. It has been a long leap from a small room in the Billerica Historical Society to the Mogan Center, but it is one of the success stories of the Canal Association.

Among other achievements of the Association in its brief span was to have the Shawsheen Aqueduct declared a National Historical Civil Engineering Landmark by the American Society of Civil Engineers on August 5, 1967. In 1972 the canal was placed on the National Historic Register. In 1974 when the route 129 bridge over the canal in Wilmington was rebuilt, the Association persuaded the state to restore a small section of the canal near and under the bridge. In 1976 they also hosted a meeting of the

Tom Smith, Governor Dukakis and Leonard Harmon riding on the packet, 1976.

American Canal Society. Quarterly meetings are held with programs, and the present membership, consisting of proprietors and regular members, is nearly 250.

Presidents of the MCA

1962–1972	Arthur Louis Eno (Billerica)
1972–1975	Douglas P. Adams (Charlestown)
1975–1977	Wilbar M. Hoxie (Reading)
1977–1981	Frances VerPlanck (Winchester)
1981–1983	H. Laurence Henchey, Jr. (Wakefield)
1983–1985	Nolan Jones (Winchester)
1985–1987	Paul P. Pearsall (Lowell)
1987–1990	David Allan Fitch (Billerica)
1990–1995	W. K. (Burt) VerPlanck (Winchester)
1995–	Nolan Jones (Amherst, NH)

The Woburn Canal Society

What do you do if one day you discover you have the remains of a canal in your side yard?

If you are Leonard Harmon of Woburn you organize. He sud-denly realized that the old ditch that went by his house and his neighbors houses was the empty bed of the abandoned Middlesex Canal. Harmon had grown up near the canal in Billerica and as a youngster was familiar with the Shawsheen aqueduct and had skated on the frozen canal winters.

How to protect this treasure? He was instrumental in the organization of the Woburn Canal Society in 1972. (The legal name of the Society actually is The Middlesex Canal Historical and Preservation Society of Woburn, Inc.) The Society is a non-profit preservation group. Its membership consists of some of the abutting property owners of the canal. They held frequent family get-togethers to clean up the canal. They also secured a section of the canal leading up to Route 128. So from Kilby Street in Woburn to Lowell street and then passing the Ramada Inn to Route 128, this part of the canal is protected. A good section of the canal here is filled with water. The bridge which takes traffic over the the canal to the Inn and the cinema complex was designed and built according to the Society's specifications.

Harmon was also for some years chair of the Woburn Historical Commission. When the Loammi Baldwin mansion was sold to developers and it looked like it would be torn down, they intervened and by much hard work saved the mansion, although it had to be moved to the other side of Route 38. The mansion had been built in 1661 by Henry Baldwin and was altered to its present appearance by his great-grandson, Loammi Baldwin, the builder of the Middlesex Canal. Today it still stands beside the old canal and serves the public as a popular restaurant.

In the 1970s, the Woburn Historical Commission persuaded the mayor to put the watered stretch of the canal which runs unbroken from the restaurant to School Street in North Woburn under its protection. With much labor and hard work Harmon and a group of volunteers cleared this stretch of the canal of un-

*Lisa Harmon leading the horse pulling the packet along
the canal behind the Baldwin mansion, 1976.*

dergrowth and restored the old tow path. As a contribution to the American bicentennial in 1976, the Commission undertook the building of a replica of a typical packet canal boat. Construction began in the Christmas season of 1975 at the Woburn Public Works building. Chairman Harmon was assisted by Tom Smith, Niles Blackburn, Dick Curran, Frank Harris, Jim Hallet, and members of the Woburn Canal Society. They worked almost every night and most weekends. At various times, members of the Middlesex Canal Association and the Department of Public Works personnel gave them a hand. They estimate that well over 3000 volunteer hours were spent in the building of the boat, plus uncounted hours devoted to design, planning, methodization, and the purchase of materials.

The hull frame of the boat, called the *Colonel Baldwin* was of white oak. Spruce was used instead of pine in the planking since present day pine is too knotty for such purposes. Instead of the original iron nails, they used more than 1400 galvanized screws. The gunwales and exterior decks are all of rough-cut oak, and the cabin is of pine. Its dimensions are 40 feet 3 inches long, 9 and a half foot beam, a height of 8 feet, and, when unloaded, a draft of six inches. The boat has a seating capacity of 40 and was launched in 1976. A film was made documenting the entire process of building this boat from felling the trees in the forest to the eventual launching of the completed craft.

For several summers they offered rides in the boat during July and August. The horse-drawn trip ran from the restaurant along the canal up to School Street and back. The trip covered more than a mile and the packet was towed by one of the two horses owned by Mr. Harmon, either "Lightfoot" or "Thunderbolt." The horses were named after two noted highwaymen, Captain Thunderbolt and Captain Lightfoot, who once plied their notorious trade along turnpikes and highways of New England.

Harmon's daughter Lisa was mounted on the horse drawing the packet and his son Keith handled the tiller of the boat. In its first season, the boat carried over 2000 passengers on the weekend excursions between July 3rd and Labor Day, indicating the popularity of the quiet glide along the old canal. Attendance continued high the next several summers also. The rides attracted much media attention and resulted in favorable publicity for the canal and its potential. After five seasons, the boat was drydocked for repairs.

For ten years, the boat was stored outside at the pumping station at Horn Pond where it suffered from the weather and lack of funding. In the fall of 1992, the Woburn Lion's Club refurbished the boat, inside and out, and, mounted on a flatbed trailer, it starred in Woburn's 350th anniversary parade. Since then it has been on display in Kiwanis Park opposite the Baldwin Mansion.

This small park was jointly created by the Historical and Conservation Commissions . It is called Kiwanis Park because of that civic group's involvement in its development and upkeep. The imposing statue of Colonel Baldwin (1745-1807) erected by his descendants in 1917 stands across from this park with the cannon that came from Fort Strong, a War of 1812 fortification designed and constructed by the Colonel's son, Loammi 2nd, for the defense of Boston against the British. A short distance beyond the park on route 38 is the 1790 House, now in commercial use, but preserved. It was built by Colonel Baldwin for his friend Count Rumford, who never made use of it. It was the scene of the celebration of the canal's opening on Dec, 31, 1803.

The Middlesex Canal Commission

But undoubtedly the most important role that Leonard Harmon played in the history of the canal was in the organization of the

Relocated Baldwin Mansion, now a fine restaurant. (Dahill photo, 1995)

Middlesex Canal Commission. The idea for this originated with Mr. Harmon, and he and Tom Smith, drew up many of the details. The plan was sponsored in the state legislature by Woburn's representative Nicholas Paleologos, adopted by the General Court as chapter 403 in 1977, and signed by Governor Michael Dukakis. Shortly before signing the legislation Governor Dukakis had visited the Woburn restoration and taken a brief ride on the packet boat.

The Commission was a mix of state officials, regional agencies, and appointed members from each of the towns the canal passed through. Its objective was to restore awareness and public use of the canal property to the extent feasible under prevailing conditions. Among other projects they were authorized to develop plans for the establishment of a Middlesex Canal Heritage Park.

Leonard Harmon was elected chair of the Commission and they proceeded promptly to their tasks. Once funding was secured they hired the Industrial Archaeology Associates of Andover to survey the canal route, to prepare maps, and present findings and recommendations to the Canal Commission. The report was completed by November 1979.

Based on this report a feasibility study was made of the Middlesex Canal Heritage Park by the Metropolitan Area Planning Council and the Northern Middlesex Area Commission (now the Northern Middlesex Council of Governments). This was completed by August 1980. These reports emphasized the need for identifying signs of the canal route in each town. They also recommended recreational use of the canal route to include bikeways, walkways, and hiking trails. Stabilization of the existing portions of the canal was considered important. And the major recommendation was for the establishment of a Heritage Park at the Concord mill pond site in North Billerica. However, lack of funding prevented their immediate implementation of most of these projects.

Meanwhile, the Commission turned to the need for better signage and designed, then placed bronze markers on granite stanchions in each of the nine communities the canal passed through. By 1997, all of the bronze plaques had been installed and dedicated.

Now entering the second phase of its work, the Canal Commission, under the leadership of Thomas Raphael of Winchester, is building on the excellent base already developed. They will be using these invaluable reports as their outline for the future development of canal activities. The new commission is tackling the major task of securing funding for the implementation of the

Canal listed on National Register.

proposed plans. Specific funds have been allocated for canal restoration in the Federal Highway Administration Enhancement Plans.

Major objectives will be to acquire all possible land, structures, and rights of way; build a continuous walkway along the canal route; restore all existing and available sites and structures; establish formal and informed interpretative centers; and establish the Heritage Park and Museum at the Billerica mill pond as the major focal point of the canal. In its bicentennial years the future looks hopeful for the old canal.

Monument in Kiwanis Park, Woburn

Cover of the Middlesex Canal Heritage Park Feasibility Study.

Stereo view of remants of Red Lock, Billerica, date unknown. (Morgan Library, Lowell)

Reconstruction of how Shawsheen Aqueduct looked at 3 different periods.

Sources

General

The major sources are the papers of the Middlesex Canal Proprietors now kept at the Mogan Center, in Lowell. These have been wonderfully indexed by Thomas C. Proctor in 1984. Additions are continually being made to the collection.

The basic study is by Christopher Roberts, *The Middlesex Canal, 1793-1860*. Cambridge, Harvard University Press, 1938.

An excellent supplement is Lewis M. Lawrence, *The Middlesex Canal*. Boston, Self-published, 1942. Reprinted 1997.

A popular account is that by Mary Stetson Clarke, *The Old Middlesex Canal*. Melrose, MA, 1974. Reprinted 1987.

A recent addition to the Mogan Center collection is Douglas P. Adams, *River in the Sky*. Charlestown, MA, Self-published and undated but ca. 1971? This 58 page account is full of generalizations and a fair number of inaccuracies and needs to be used with caution. But he has some interesting items, though the source is not given. For example, his title comes, he says, from an "urchin, staring up at barges crossing the Shawsheen aqueduct, barely visible from the Shawsheen bridge below," and seeing what he thought was "a river in the sky." (p. 17). Another unsourced story is of an old boatman replying to the question "Plenty of drunkenness among the workmen?" with the response, "Bless your heart, no! Mr. Eddy (later superintendent) didn't put up with no drunkards on the canal. They could drink all night, sir, and be steady as an eight-day clock in the morning." (p. 21).

Front Matter

The names of some of the workers on the canal are taken from a variety of sources: Colonel Baldwin's diary, Christopher Robert's book, Lewis Lawrence's book, but principally from a Roll Book found in the Woburn Public Library. We took a sampling of over a hundred names from this book to reprint on our cover. In all cases we used the spelling as given in the book, thus, "Daniel Got" instead of "Daniel Gott."

A Jaunt to Horn Pond

There are three accounts of this trip to Horn Pond on July 18, 1817. One is the letter of Ms. Fanny Searle to Mrs. Margaret Curzon written from Brookline on July 20, 1817 and found in

Colonial Society of Massachusetts. Publications, Vol. 7, Cambridge, MA 1905. pp. 6-12.

The second is an extract from the Journal of Miss Eliza Susan Quincy under the date of July 18, 1817 and found in the same work on pp. 12-14. The third account is in the *Memoir of Samuel Joseph May*, by Thomas James Mumford. Boston, American Unitarian Association, 1882. pp. 37-39. We have amalgamated them in our version here.

Only the journal of Eliza Quincy, written the same day as the event, tells us that George Emerson joined his friend May in gathering the flowers. Even May's biography, written so many years later, does not credit him with his gallantry.

Bringing New Hampshire to Boston

This account is a fictional version of many an actual voyage of a raft of logs from New Hampshire, down the Merrimack River and onto the Middlesex Canal to Charlestown.

How the Canal Was Born

Who first conceived the idea of the Middlesex Canal? There is no clear documentary evidence now available. As Christopher Roberts carefully notes in his book the idea is "attributed" to John Sullivan. But this attribution first appears in Amory's biography of Sullivan written in 1859. This may represent valid family tradition.

But the great preponderance of Medford men associated with the original petition to the General Court allows the speculation that perhaps the idea might have been conceived in Medford. For certainly the early plans were all for the canal to end in Medford.

With so many of the Hall family involved, could it have been one of the Halls? Unless some conclusive evidence turns up we shall never know.

In any case, the Medford men needed someone of Sullivan's expertise and skill to secure passage of the legislation establishing the corporation. And if indeed he was a latecomer to the project and not its originator, he certainly became its most enthusiastic supporter and promoter until the end of his life. We have not tried to solve the mystery, but have accepted the attribution that the idea originated with Sullivan.

Note that the canal as originally planned and the finished canal are not the same. The Samuel Thompson survey shows three canals comprising the original Middlesex Canal. Extensive use was to be made of natural waterways, ponds, and rivers. This, of course, is what the proprietors asked him to survey in 1794. The canal was to end in Medford, or more accurately in Symmes River in what is now Winchester, but then was still Woburn. From there boats would proceed down the Symmes river, enter the Mystic Lake and proceed down the Mystic river to Boston. This canal would run to Horn Pond in Woburn. Here boats would enter Horn Pond, crossing it and enter a second canal which ran to the Concord Mill Pond. From the Concord millpond they would enter a third canal that ran to the Merrimack river.

This canal is shown on a map drawn by Osgood Carleton in 1795 and now in the William L. Clements Library at the University of Michigan. A photostat of this map is in the writers' possession. It shows the contrasting Eastern and Western routes proposed for the canal, which eventually was decided in favor of the Eastern route due to the objections of the people living on the Western route.

At a much later date, the canal was changed to a single canal running from the Merrimack River into Charlestown millpond and making no use of natural rivers or lakes. There is no discussion in any document we have seen about this major change. It must have taken place verbally at meetings of the directors.

Certainly the original Medford proprietors were unhappy about the decision and as a result got permission to establish the Medford Branch canal in 1804 which permitted lumber rafts to leave the canal in Medford and reach the burgeoning shipbuilding industry on the banks of the Mystic river in that town.

Perhaps part of the decision not to use the Mystic river might have come from the fact that it was then a tidal river, and at low tide boats and rafts may not have had enough water to permit easy passage on to Boston.

The authors have seen no discussion of this major change in either the Roberts, Lawrence, or Clarke book. Support for our conclusion is found in the fact that the Peter C. Brooks land in West Medford was not purchased until 1802. The Charlestown millpond was not purchased until August 1803.

Diary of a Dig

The dimensions of the canal as suggested by Weston were 30-1/2 feet wide across at the top, 20 feet across at the bottom, a depth of 3-1/2 feet, and a slope of 33 degrees from bottom to top.

We wonder if there might not have been some kind of a template available to the individual contractors working on different parts of the canal to make sure that these dimensions were adhered to wherever possible. (In some cases they were not.)

Would it be wrong to assume that Baldwin could have constructed what we might call a "Guide" that would represent these dimensions? Perhaps it was full size, perhaps only half size. The contractor could then use this to see if his portion of the canal was conforming to the size requirements.

We stress that this is a guess on our part and that no document or reference to such a guide can be found. Indeed, it may be that each contractor continually monitored the size requirements by some measuring stick, but this seems time-consuming, wasteful, and inaccurate.

Taming the Merrimack

We drew on the standard accounts in Roberts, Lawrence, and Clarke. But we were particularly helped by Mr. Charles Mower of Merrimack, NH. He is an expert on the present state of the canals on the Merrimack and has talked to many groups about them. He also leads expeditions on the river for people who want to see what remains. He graciously shared some of his slides with us for this work.

How the Canal Worked

This chapter is drawn from Eddy's 1835 report supplemented by general information about the canal from the standard works.

Overview

The artist's illustrations are based on George R. Baldwin's Field Notes of the 1829 survey, supplemented by maps of the period. The identifications of outstanding features of the canal are taken from the Lasher map and from the books of Roberts, Lawrence, Clarke, and VerPlanck.

Overfight

In 1979, the Industrial Archaeology Associates made an aerial survey of the canal for the Middlesex Canal Commission. This was exactly 150 years after George Baldwin made his 1829 survey. We had hoped to reproduce these photographs, but they appeared to be missing. A long search eventually turned them up in the archives of the Massachusetts Historical Commission. But they were found not to be suitable for our purposes. So instead we have relied on some aerial photographs taken by Nolan Jones, twice President of the Middlesex Canal Association. His photographs were taken in the early 1970s. These show good sections of the canal as its route is visible from the air in our time. We have overlaid his photographs with the approximate route of the canal in gold. These do not form a fully connected view of the canal from Charlestown to the Merrimack, but we begin in Medford, and omit some sections. In all he took 34 photographs and we give a sampling of major sections of the canal.

Closing Down the Canal

This chapter is based on Frothingham's reports and the general information in Roberts, Lawrence, and Clarke.

A Canal Scrapbook

Each selection in the "Scrapbook" indicates where we obtained it.

Afterglow

The diary of Edward Everett can be found in the Massachusetts Historical Society.

The full run of *Towpath Topics* gives much of the information about walkers, photographers, casual authors, etc. Our information about Roberts was largely obtained from the Archives at Duke University. Our thanks to Mr. Thomas F. Harkins for his assistance.

Our information about Lawrence came from newspapers of the time, the Melrose Public Library, and research by Burt VerPlanck. Our information about Clarke came from newspapers, the Melrose Public Library, and *Towpath Topics*.

New Life—New Interest

Information on the Middlesex Canal Association was gathered from the run of the *Towpath Topics*, and from personal interviews with Arthur Louis Eno Jr., with Fred Lawson Jr., and from the secretarial notes of Barbara Manning and her successors kept at the Mogan Center, Lowell. Mr. Lawson shared with us his 1960 account of the canal which he had prepared for a course at the University of Lowell. He also allowed us to make copies of the historic slides now in his possession.

Information about the Woburn Canal Society was obtained from personal interviews with Leonard Harmon and Tom Smith and articles in the *Towpath Topics*.

Information about the Middlesex Canal Commission was obtained from Harmon, Smith, *Towpath Topics*, and documents of the Commission.

Index

Page numbers in italics refer to illustrations.

Aberjona River, 26, 43
Adams, Douglas P., 96,123
Adams, John Quincy, 25
Adams, President John, 25
Allard, Christine C., 103
Ames, Sarah, 103
Amoskeag Canal, 50, 54
    locks on, *46*
Aqueducts
    Hale's Brook, 17
    Hale's River, 17
    River Meadow, 17
    rules for packet boat travel on, 17, 21
    Shawsheen, 16, 17, 19, 43, 106, 117
    passing Shawsheen aqueduct, *16*
    Sinking Meadow, 19

Baker, E. T., 115
Baldwin, Benjamin Franklin, 31, 34
Baldwin, Colonel Loammi, 19, 24, 27, 28,
    31, *35*, 45, 47, 50, 57, 59, 65, 89, 102,
    109, 115, 123, 125
Baldwin, Cyrus, 34

Baldwin, George R., 65, 73, 89, 99
Baldwin, James Fowle, 57, 89
Barrell, Joseph, 25
Bateman, Mr. P., 32
Beachum Landing,3
Beard, Jonathan, 35
Bell, Shubael, 95
Bennet, Catherine Wilkie, 115
Black Brook, 17, 32, 42
Blackburn, Niles, 125
Blodget, Judge Samuel, *49*, 50
Blodget's Canal, 50, 54
Boott, Kirk, 88
Bow Canal, 52
Bowers, John, 48
Boyd, Pliny Steele, 48
Brooks Peter Chardon, 4, 25, 43, 99, 100
Brooks, Edward, 113

Carleton, Osgood, 26
Carney, Edward, 116, 119
Charles River, 21, 23, 26, 59, 95
Charlestown mill pond, 3, 10, 21, 26, 45

Charlestown mill pond, 2
Cheney, G., 102
Clarke, Edwin, 118
Clarke, Mary Stetson, 118
Collester, Clinton H., 117
Colson, Israel, 59, 60, 63
Concord millpond, 26
Concord River, 17, 24, 25, 31, 32, 35, 37,
    39, 42, 43, 59, 91, 103, 104
Connecticut River, 23, 24
Converse, Parker L., 102
Coolidge, Baldwin, 109, 115
Cornhill, 21
Coverly, Edith, 116
Cowing, Daniel, 103
Cowing, Micajah, 103
Cromwell's Canal, 48
Cross, Mr., 32
Curran, Dick, 125

Dalton, Madame, 104
Darwin, Dr. Erasmus, 102
Davis, Isaac O., 88

Delaware River, 23
Dickens, Charles, 90
Doggett, John, 87
Dowse, Benjamin, 37, 43
Dukakis, Governor Michael, 122, 127
Duncan, William, 52
Dutch trass, 38
Dykeman, Mrs. Wendell, 115

Eddy, Albert, 61
Eddy, Caleb, 57-63, 87, 89, 90, 91, 117
Eddy, Caroline, 61
Eddy, Mary Baker, 53
Emerson, George, 3, 8
Emerson, Ralph Waldo, 3
Eno, Arthur L. Jr., 121, 123
Erie Canal, 116
Everen, Van Mr., 116
Everett, Edward, 113

Faden, James L., 115
Falls
    Amoskeag, 47, 49, 50, 51
    Billerica, 104
    Bow, 47
    Cohas, 47, 49, 54
    Cromwell, 47, 49, 54
    Garven, 47, 52
    Goff, 47, 49, 50, 54
    Griffin, 47, 49, 54
    Merrill's, 47, 49, 54
    Moor, 47, 49
    Sewall's, 48

    Short, 47, 49, 54
    Turkey, 47, 52
    Wicasee, 47

Field, Eldred, 121
Fitch, David Allen, 123
Frothingham, Richard, 58, 87-92

Gardner locks, 6
Gay, Prof. Edwin F., 117
Gillis' Lock, 19, 103
Gilson's Lock, 4, 10, 114, 115
Gore, Christopher, 25

Hadley, Sam Jr., 61, 62, 63
Hadley, Sam Sr., 61, 62, 63
Hall, Benjamin, 31, 45
Hall, Dorothy I., 119
Hall, Nathaniel, 45
Hall, Richard, 45
Hallet, Jim, 125
Hancock Governor John, 24, 25
Harmon, Leonard, 123, 125, 127
Harper, Walter, 118
Harris, Frank, 125
Henchey, H. Lawrence Jr., 123
Hills, John, 32
Hollis Lock, 6
Hooksett Canal, 52
Horn Pond House, 6, 7
    Horn Pond house, 7
Horn Pond, 3, 6, 17, 21, 23, 24, 26, 31,
    37, 45, 57, 102, 114, 125

Hoxie, Wilbar M., 123
Hudson River, 23
Huffmasters Bridge, 6

Ipswich River, 31
Isle of Hooksett Canal, Proprietors of, 52

Jackson, Patrick Tracy, 88, 89
Jacobs, Mary Morey, 118
Jaques Mill, 31
Jaques, Samuel, 28, 32, 34, 35, 37, 45
Jarvis, Leonard, 43
Jones, Nolan, 73, 123
Joy, Benjamin, 25

King, Samuel, 113
Knox, General, 32

Lake Champlain, 24
Lake of the Woods, 6, 19
Lake Sunapee, 24
Landing Number 1, 21
Lasher, Harry J., 119
Lawrence, Lewis M., 106, 118
Lincoln, Abraham, 47
Linscott, Louis R., 115
Locks
    how they work, 33
    Lock Number 1, 21
    length of locks, 45
    Horn Pond, 94
    Middlesex Village, 105
Loring, John F., 88

Lubber Brook, 19
Lyman, George W., 88

Magoun, Thatcher, 45
Mann, Moses W., 113, 115
Manning, Timothy, 37
Maple Meadow River, 31
May, Samuel, 8
McGregor, Robert, 52
Medford Bridge, 31
Medford Pond, 31
Medford Shipyards, 4
Merrill, Morison, 116
Merrimack River, 12, 14, 17, 23, 24, 26,
    31, 32, 35, 37, 39, 42, 43, 44, 45, 47,
    54, 59, 73, 95, 105, 106
Middlesex Village, 31, 21
Middlesex Canal
    agent of, 87
    amount of business done on the canal
        in 1805, 28
    annual reports on, 57-63
    appropriation of land for, 26, 27
    association goals, 121
    Boston and Lowell Rail-Road Corpora-
        tion, 88
    building of canal, 48-53
        Canal Corporation, 23, 24, 99
    dimensions of, 35
    Committee on Rail-ways and Canals, 88
    completion of, 27
    completion of Merrimack end, 42
    daily number of passengers, 89

East and West Middlesex Canal Town-
    ships, 106
efforts to save, 113
first superintendent of, 31
fishing in, 96, 97, 100, 101-102, 113
hiring of workers, 34
initial cost estimate of, 32
initial survey of, 24, 25, 26, 31, 107
Iron Horse, 87
landing fees, 21
last trip on, 91, 113
main source of water, 17
Medford Branch Canal and Locks, 45
Middlesex Canal Commission, 73, 125
Middlesex Canal Historical and Preser-
    vation Society of Woburn, Inc., 123,
    124
Middlesex Canal Proprietors, 45, 48,
    50, 52, 106
Moosehead townships, 107
muskrats/minks effect on leaks, 113,
    58, 59, 62
muskrats, bounty on, 62
official termination of, 88
opposition to, 34
original vision of, 26, 48
packet boats, 3, 4, 6, 17
passports, 14, 21, 58, 59
photos of, 115-116
potential canal route from Boston to
    Montreal, 26
preventing water leakage, 37-38
proprietors opposition to railroads, 88

railroads impact on closing, 87
raising money to build, 49-50
reasons for building, 23, 47
reasons for closing, 87
shares in, 25, 27, 91
shutting down and closing of, 87
summit of, 17
swimming and skating in, 101, 102, 113
tolls, 13, 14, 21, 58, 60, 90, 91
tools used in construction of, 38
total cost of, 45
tow-line, 95-96
townships, 106
trade expansion as a result of, 24
use of horses with, 3, 14, 19
water usage on, 105-106
West Middlesex Canal Township, 107
Middlesex Water Company, 90
Middlesex Canal Association, 115, 116,
    119, 121, 122, 125
Morey, Charles F., 115, 118
Morey, Samuel, 119
Munro, Melville, 115
Mystic Lake, 11, 21, 26, 31, 35, 59, 99
Mystic Pond, 4, 6, 8, 37
Mystic River, 4, 21, 23, 24, 25, 26, 27, 30,
    31, 44, 99, 115
    building the aqueduct over the Mystic
        River, Medford, 31

Nashua River, 24
Nichol's Lock, 19
Northern Dept., 35

Otis, Senator Harrison Gray, 60
Ox-bow bend, 19

Page, Jonathan, 96, 97
Paleologos, Nicholas, 127
Parker, Daniel, 88
Parker, Ichabod, 34
Parkman, Samuel, 25, 95
Passing Pond, 6
Payro, Joseph C., 116
Pearsall, Paul P., 123
Pemigewasset River, 47
Ploughed Hill, 3
Pope, Lemuel, 88
Procter, Thomas C., 122

Quincy, Eliza, 8
Quincy, Josiah, 3, 60

Raphael, Thomas, 127
Rawson, Michael J., 99
Rembert, Helen Pauline, 118
Revolutionary War, 4, 6
Richardson, Abel, 31
Richardson, Thomas, 34
River Meadow, 17, 32, 39
Roberts, Christopher, 117-119
Roberts, Garrett, 118
Roberts, Weldon, 118
Rogers, Oliver W., 106
Royall house, 9, 21
Royall, Colonel Isaac, 4

Sandy Pond, 32
Shawsheen River, 17, 19, 32, 43
Sheldon, C. Talbot, 104
Sheldon, Harry G., 103, 115
Smith, Tom, 107, 125, 127
Snow, Joseph, 42
Southern Dept., 35, 37
St. Lawrence River, 24
Stark, Colonel, 4
Stark, General George, 53
Stetson, Thomas M., 101
Stoddard Locks, 6
Struik, Prof. Dirk J., 117
Sullivan, Governor John, 25, 28
    Governor John Sullivan, 25
Sullivan, J. L., 96
Sullivan, James, 23-28, 42
Sullivan, John L., 3, 4, 8
Sullivan, John Langton, 28, 48
Sullivan, Judge, 44
Sullivan's Harbor, 42
Symmes River, 4, 24

The Great Swamp, 17
Thompson, Jonathan, 35
Thompson, Samuel, 25, 31, 32
Thoreau, Henry David, 104
Tidd, Marshall, 115
Touro, Abraham, 25
Tuck, Judith, 97
Tuck, Samuel Jones, 97

Union Canal, 50

Verplanck, Frances, 123
Verplanck, W. K., 123

Warner River, 24
Washington, George, 4
Waters, Rev. Wilson, 104
Webster, Daniel, 3, 8, 88
Weir Bridge, 31
Weston, William, 32, 34, 35, 37
Whistler, George W., 89
Wicasee Canal, 48
Wilson, Daniel, 59, 60, 63
Winooski River, 24
Winnipesaukee River, 47
Winthrop, Judge James, 24, 28, 31, 34
Wood, Mal, 116
Wyman, Jeremiah, 37
Wyman, Paul, 37
Wyman, Zeb, 37